PRACTICAL SOCIAL WORK

Series Editor: Jo Campling

BASW

Editorial Advisory Board:
Robert Adams, Terry Bamford, Charles Barker,
Lena Dominelli, Malcolm Payne, Michael Preston-Shoot,
Daphne Statham and Jane Tunstill

Social work is at an important stage in its development. All professions must be responsive to changing social and economic conditions if they are to meet the needs of those they serve. This series focuses on sound practice and the specific contribution which social workers can make to the well-being of our society.

The British Association of Social Workers has always been conscious of its role in setting guidelines for practice and in seeking to raise professional standards. The conception of the Practical Social Work series arose from a survey of BASW members to discover where they, the practitioners in social work, felt there was the most need for new literature. The response was overwhelming and enthusiastic, and the result is a carefully planned, coherent series of books. The emphasis is firmly on practice set in a theoretical framework. The books will inform, stimulate and promote discussion, thus adding to the further development of skills and high professional standards. All the authors are practitioners and teachers of social work representing a wide variety of experience.

JO CAMPLING

A list of published titles in this series follows overleaf

Practical Social Work
Series Standing Order ISBN 0–333–69347–7

You can receive future titles in this series as they are published by placing a standing order. Please contact your bookseller or, in the case of difficulty, write to us at the address below with your name and address, the title of the series and the ISBN quoted above.

Customer Services Department, Macmillan Distribution Ltd
Houndmills, Basingstoke, Hampshire RG21 6XS, England

PRACTICAL SOCIAL WORK

Working with Young Offenders

Second Edition

John Pitts

First edition 1990
Reprinted three times
Second edition 1999

Published by
MACMILLAN PRESS LTD
Houndmills, Basingstoke, Hampshire RG21 6XS
and London
Companies and representatives
throughout the world

ISBN 0–333–68265–3

A catalogue record for this book is available
from the British Library.

This book is printed on paper suitable for
recycling and made from fully managed and
sustained forest sources.

10   9   8   7   6   5   4   3   2   1
08   07   06   05   04   03   02   01   00   99

Printed in Malaysia

Contents

List of Tables

Preface to the Second Edition

When I wrote the first edition of this book, in the late 1980s, young offenders were still the responsibility of local authority field social workers Because of this, the first edition of *Working with Young Offenders* was aimed, largely, at field social workers who might, from time to time, work with children and young people in trouble with the law, and local authority youth justice workers.

Today, workers with young offenders are specialists not generalists, even though they may be drawn from education, the health service, the police, the education service, the local authority social services department or specialist voluntary sector programmes. With the implementation of the Crime and Disorder Act (1998), they also have a great deal more power and responsibility. And so in this new edition of *Working with Young Offenders* I have tried to address these changes in the administration of youth justice, the role of youth justice workers and the substantial changes in the law which have occurred since the first edition was published.

I have been helped enormously in this task by the youth justice workers, youth workers, police officers, social workers and the magistrate who attended my youth justice and community safety seminars at the University of Luton's Vauxhall Centre for the Study of Crime. At the Centre Alan Marlow and David Porteous have given me many valuable ideas about community safety and youth victimisation, which I have gratefully integrated into this book. Charley Burr, the co-ordinator of the Camden Investing in Young People Initiative, has revealed to me how the youth justice and community safety provision of the Crime and Disorder Act (1998) can be made to work in unison to benefit children and young people in trouble. The chapters on preventive work have benefited enormously from Charley's wise counsel.

I began to write the second edition of *Working With Young Offenders* just before the 1997 election. This was the worst possible time to start, since government policy and the law were both in a state of flux. That I stuck with the task is a testimony to the encouragement, the sound advice, the wealth of material supplied by, and my discussions with, Mike Thomas, Chair of the National Association for Youth Justice and Head of Luton's Youth Offending Team. He kept telling me that youth justice workers needed a book like this. I hope he was right.

JOHN PITTS

1

The Politics of Policy

Youth justice in the 1980s and 1990s

The erratic twists and turns in the politics, policy and practice of youth justice since 1979 have had little to do with the changing shape of youth crime during the period. They are better understood as a product of governmental attempts to manage the tensions between its political ideology, economic reality and the desire to be re-elected. This has meant that the issue of youth crime has sometimes occupied the centre of the political stage, most notably in the early 1980s, the early 1990s and 1997, while at others it has been pushed out of the political limelight and placed in the hands of the 'experts'.

1979–82: the restoration of the rule of law

For a time, Margaret Thatcher's first term in office looked as if it might also be her last. The economic recession deepened and unemployment soared, giving the lie to promises of new freedoms and greater prosperity. Faced with this situation, the government attempted to deflect public attention away from the economy and onto crime and, in doing so, to present itself as the only party with the moral and political grit to 'win the war' against it.

At the heart of Conservative criminal justice rhetoric between 1979 and 1982 was the commitment to the restoration of 'the rule of the law' and the pledge to render the streets of Britain safe, once more, for law-abiding citizens (Hall *et al.*, 1978; Lea and Young, 1984; Pitts, 1996). The 1982 Criminal Justice Act (CJA) was heralded as the law which, by restoring the powers of the police and the bench, would make good Mrs Thatcher's 'law and order' promises. Yet, behind the scenes, it was clear that the youth justice system inherited by the Thatcher government was a mess; an incoherent mixture of welfare-oriented measures introduced by the Children and Young Persons Act (1969) and the attendance centres, detention centres and borstals of a previous era. It was a system which was locking up more and more less difficult children and young people. This was forcing older juveniles up into the adult system where they were placing enormous strains on a prison system which was itself at bursting point. Moreover, youth justice was one of the many areas of government spending perceived to be spiralling out of control and this was acutely embarrassing for an administration committed to 'small government' and 'good housekeeping' (Scull, 1977).

1982–92: the fiscal crisis and decarceration

Having been saved from electoral defeat by the Falklands war, the second Thatcher administration, now in the thrall of monetarism, confronted the reality of Britain's fiscal crisis (Scull, 1977). The crisis centred upon the inability of the state to maintain existing welfare and crime control services in the face of rising costs, competing demands on state expenditure, largely from unemployment benefit, mounting political pressure to reduce taxation and a significant reduction in the tax-paying population. As a result, the period between 1982 and 1992 witnessed a sustained attempt to contain the burgeoning costs of crime control and the penal system. This led to the development, by Home Secretaries Brittan, Hurd, Waddington and Baker, of a highly pragmatic strategy of 'delinquency management' rooted in a profound scepticism about the efficacy of imprisonment or the possibility of rehabilitation outside it. Thus the 1982 CJA, its blood-curdling rhetoric notwithstanding, was the law which initiated the rationalisation of the youth justice system in England and Wales.

An uneasy alliance

In 1983, the DHSS launched the Intermediate Treatment Initiative in which £15 000 000 was committed to the provision of 4500 alternatives to custody over the following three years. The uneasy alliance, between the youth justice lobby comprising youth justice professionals, penal reform groups, progressive Home Office civil servants and academics, and a neo-conservative law and order government, which the Initiative required, yielded some remarkable results. Between 1981 and 1989, the numbers of juveniles imprisoned in young offenders institutions fell from 7700 to 1900 per annum.

The Initiative succeeded because the desire of the youth justice lobby to limit the state's intervention in the lives of children and young people in trouble articulated with the government's cost-cutting imperatives and its commitment to 'small government'. Besides, for the neo-conservatives who were gaining increasing influence within government, the state had no mandate to intervene in the social causes of crime. If the problem was to be solved at all, it would be solved by punishing serious criminals harshly and sending those on the threshold of crime an unequivocal message about the consequences of their actions. Thus, in Britain, prior to 1992, ministers chose to send these unequivocal messages to young offenders in community-based alternatives to custody. Many members of the conservative government were aware that the social changes wrought by neo-conservative economic policy probably fostered youth crime, but such was the power of neo-conservative ideology in the mid-1980s that there was a tacit acceptance that this was a price worth paying. In consequence the government opted for the manipulation of the apparatus of justice and crime control and the media rather than social intervention in high-crime neighbourhoods.

Political dissonance

There was, of course, a considerable ideological distance between the pessimistic, and apparently quiescent, governmental stance on youth crime in Britain in the 1980s and that of the traditionally punitive rank and file of the Conservative Party. The bridge was provided by the 'justice model' which began life as a strategic alternative to traditional forms of social work intervention with young people in trouble in the 1970s (Thorpe *et al.*, 1980). The justice model was sold to the key political, professional and media constituencies as a tough, confrontational, non-custodial response to 'high-tariff' offenders, the scientific validity of which was vouchsafed by cognitive psychology. The justice model accorded closely with both the administrative and political imperatives of contemporary government criminal justice strategy. The administrative fit was achieved by an individualised of mode of correctional 'treatment', the timing of which was endlessly elastic, determined by the length of the community-based penalty imposed upon the 'young offender'. The political fit was vouchsafed by the treatment's obvious remoralising objectives and its claims to effect sustainable behavioural change.

It is at least doubtful that either the youth justice lobby or Home Office ministers actually believed that the justice model 'worked'. Thus their involvement in the manipulation of ideas and the reproduction of correctional practices was essentially pragmatic. Both sides chose to live in this state of 'bad faith' because the alliance they had entered was working so well for both parties that to 'rock the boat' by revealing the fiction which underlay the endeavour would have been strategic suicide.

The new penology

The youth justice system which had emerged in England and Wales by the late 1980s contained many of the characteristics of what Feeley and Simon (1992) call the 'new penology'. They write:

> The new penology is neither about punishing nor rehabilitating individuals. It is about identifying and managing unruly groups. It is concerned with the rationality not of individual behaviour or even community organisation, but of managerial processes. Its goal is not to eliminate crime but to make it tolerable through systemic co-ordination . . . For example, although parole and probation have long been justified as a means of reintegrating offenders into the community, increasingly they are being seen as cost-effective ways of imposing long-term management on the dangerous. (1992, pp. 453–4)

The technology of the new penology, as it developed in Britain, consisted of *risk of custody scales*, which enabled practitioners to calculate the severity of the alternatives to custody they should propose to the courts; *the combination order*, ushered in by the 1991 CJA which gave the new youth courts, which it also brought into being, flexibility in specifying the content of such alternatives; *the justice model* which offered an ideologically acceptable rehabilitative practice; the requirement upon practitioners, under the 1991 Act, to assess the *dangerousness and future risk* posed by the offender, and longer periods of toughened *post-release supervision*.

Reform by stealth

The youth justice lobby had chosen to remain silent about the growing poverty, victimisation and social polarisation occurring in the high-crime neighbourhoods from which the bulk of adjudicated young offenders were drawn. They had done so because of their fear that, if the issues of falling youth custody rates and burgeoning youth crime were brought together, a causal connection might be made and a new 'crusade' against youth crime, emanating from the government's back benches and the media, might be set in train. By 1991 it appeared that their restraint was to be rewarded. The 1991 CJA marked the moment when the lessons learnt in the development of youth justice in the 1980s were to be enshrined in law and translated into the adult justice system. The 1991 Criminal Justice Act and the Children Act 1989, taken together, constituted a progressive moment in the post-war history of youth justice in the UK. The Children Act gave statutory recognition to the importance of avoiding prosecution wherever possible and to the fact that the young offender was also a 'child in need', while the 1991 Act, and subsequent Home Office Circular (30/92) drew the attention of sentencers to sect. 44 of the Children and Young Persons Act 1933 (C&YPA) which states that 'all courts must have regard to the welfare of children and young people who appear before them'. The Act brought 17-year-olds into the ambit of the newly created youth court which, with the new family proceedings court, replaced the juvenile court. The maximum period a young person could spend in a young offenders institution was reduced to one year. However, the greatest prize the 1991 Criminal Justice Act appeared to offer penal reformers, one which had eluded them throughout the century, was the cessation of the imprisonment of children under the age of 15.

1992–6: the repoliticisation of youth justice

However, their optimism was to be short-lived. In 1992 there were riots in Bristol, Salford and Burnley, which revived the anxieties generated by the 1991 riots in Oxford, Cardiff and Tyneside. In Manchester a 14-year-old bystander was shot dead in the Moss Side 'crack wars' and in London a 12-year-old was stabbed in his school playground. Ram-raiding and 'twocking' were in the headlines and John Major's Conservative government, recently weakened by a narrow electoral victory, was under attack from the Labour Party on their law and order record. Labour made great play of the fact that youth crime was running out of control and that the traditional 'party of law and order' was unwilling and unable to contain it. And then two-year-old James Bulger was brutally murdered by two truanting 10-year-olds. The political storm which accompanied this murder, and the ensuing trial, focused national attention on the government's capacity to discharge its most important responsibility and fulfil the primary rationale for its very existence, the maintenance of social order. The Major government was under growing pressure to find a new idea and a new policy.

The renaissance of youth imprisonment

Only five months after their implementation, the key reforms of the 1991 Criminal Justice Act were reversed when Home Secretary Kenneth Clark announced his plans to reintroduce custody for 12–15-year-olds in secure training centres. In his hastily constructed Criminal Justice Act (1993) Clarke also reversed the requirement in the 1991 Act that details of previous convictions should not be taken into account by youth court magistrates in reaching their sentencing decisions. Hot on its heels came the Criminal Justice and Public Order Act (1994) which introduced the 'secure training order' for 12–15-year-olds. The 1994 Act also doubled the amount of time a young offender could spend in a young offenders institution and extended the provisions of sect. 53 of the 1933 C&YPA, which relates to children and young people convicted of grave crimes, to younger offenders aged 10–13. These changes led to an increase in both the number and the length of custodial sentences imposed on children and young people. Between 1992 and 1997 the numbers of juveniles sentenced to custody rose from 3900 to 6200 (Home Office, 1998c).

In 1994 the Home Secretary, Michael Howard, set about toughening the probation service by allowing direct recruitment of ex-NCOs and police officers and severing probation's traditional links with social work education. Taking inspiration from some of the more punitive practices within the US correctional system, in February 1995 he announced plans for 'tougher and more demanding' 'house of pain' regimes, 'aimed at knocking criminal tendencies out of young offenders' (*The Times*, 5/2/95). With this melange of toughened teenage prison regimes and new rehabilitations enshrined in a new, more restrictive, more punitive Criminal Justice Act, Michael Howard set about restoring the electoral fortunes of the Conservative Party.

These changes dealt a severe blow to the delinquency management strategies of the 1980s and signalled a new era in which crime in general, and youth crime in particular, were to be repoliticised and moved back to the centre of the political stage. Home Secretary Michael Howard's beliefs about the benefits of the measures he had introduced were, famously, articulated at the Conservative Party conference in October 1993 where he observed:

> Prison works, it ensures that we are protected from murderers, muggers and rapists – and it makes many who are tempted to commit crime think twice . . . This may mean that many more people will go to prison. I do not flinch from that. We shall no longer judge the success of our system of justice by a fall in our prison population.

Howard's Crime (Sentences) Bill (1996) introduced into the UK forms of mandatory sentencing akin to the notorious 'three-strikes' strategy which had been pursued in several US states. In 1999, Labour's Home Secretary Jack Straw announced that the '3-strikes' strategy was to be introduced for juvenile and adult burglars.

The professional backlash

With the major reforms of the 1991 Criminal Justice Act either shelved or unimplemented, and realising that the Conservatives were probably facing defeat in the forthcoming general election, in the mid-1990s the Principal Youth Justice Officers of Inner London came together with the Inner London Probation Service and the Association of Directors of Social Services to produce a *Statement of Principles and Practice Standards for Youth Justice* (ILYJS, 1995).

This proved to be the first move in a train of events which culminated in the development of a set of national standards and principles for youth justice in England and Wales. The document recognised the uneven nature of youth service and educational and welfare provision from borough to borough and the inconsistencies in sentencing between different youth courts. It therefore asserted that every young person who offends or is at risk of offending should have access to:

- services which help to stop them becoming involved, or further involved, in offending through equal access to high quality services;
- equal treatment in the criminal justice system irrespective of their race, gender, sexual orientation, cultural or religious background;
- provision which helps them to develop into well-adjusted adults;
- services to help them remain, wherever possible, in their community and with their family.

The statements of standards represented an attempt to both rectify current anomalies and injustices and flesh out a humane, evidence-based approach to youth crime and justice which, the authors believed, would be congruent with a new Labour government's stance on these issues.

New Labour, new danger?

In the run-up to the 1997 general election, there was considerable speculation about whether New Labour's apparent 'toughness' on youth crime was simply a way of stealing the issue of 'law and order' from the Conservatives. Indeed many youth justice professionals believed that behind the electoral window dressing was a government in waiting which would be both more compassionate and more intelligent in its dealings with children and young people in trouble with the law. Once elected, it became evident that New Labour meant what it had said.

American dreams

New Labour's electoral strategy was borrowed, more or less lock, stock and barrel, from Bill Clinton for whom it secured an unprecedented two terms as Democratic president. Thus the harsh tones of New Labour in its discussion of young offenders may be seen as a product of what the American sociologist William Julius Wilson has described as the 'suburbanisation' of political life. Like the new Democrats in the USA, New Labour appeared to believe that it no longer needed to make concessions to the inhabitants of the inner cities, or the council estates on the ring roads, to win elections. They calculated that those working class people in the cities who could still be bothered to vote would probably vote Labour anyway. But to win and maintain power they had to win the suburbs, the places where real electoral power resided. If 'Worcester Woman' was to permanently change her voting habits, New Labour reasoned, she must be made to feel that a Labour government would contain the threat posed to her property, person and peace of mind, not to mention the educational opportunities of her children, by the roughly spoken, badly behaved young people who haunt the streets of the inner city and the estates on the edge of town. And New Labour reassured her that they would do just this:

> Schools require a new, much tougher, set of disciplinary sanctions to deal with unruly and uncooperative pupils – such as compulsory homework on school premises, weekend and Saturday night detention, and the banning of favourite leisure pursuits such as football matches.
>
> This greater emphasis on discipline should be matched in the local community. The police, schools and local authority services must work together closely to crack down on vandalism and other antisocial behaviour. Excessive tolerance of low-level subcriminal behaviour by unruly young people undermines general respect for the rule of law, ruins the environment and makes a misery of the lives of many innocent people – and provides a breeding ground for more serious crime. (Mandelson and Liddle, 1996)

The real roots of middle class anxiety in the 1990s are to be found in the social and economic consequences of the globalisation of national economies and the profound changes to traditional patterns of employment wrought by information technology. But these are factors which are usually only dimly grasped and over which modern governments have little control and, unlike troublesome youth, they do not lend themselves to easy characterisation or caricature.

Towards a punitive community

There is, however, more in play here than the crude manipulation of the anxieties of potential voters. New Labour's stance on young offenders and the conflation of bad behaviour and crime derives from, and articulates with, an emergent intellectual orthodoxy while appears to have united politically active intellectuals of all political hues. On the far right is Norman Dennis (1997) who traces a clear line from welfare dependency via excessive sexual intercourse to youth crime and public disorder. Also on the right, Charles Murray (1994), ably abetted by Andrew Neil and the *Sunday Times*, continues to pursue the link between welfare dependency and premature and profligate pregnancy on the one hand, while on the other he presents quasi-scientific proof that the effects of the increased use of imprisonment will reduce the crime rate (Murray, 1997). On what is described as the 'post-Marxist left' Beatrix Campbell (1993) points to the crisis in working class masculinity, coupled with police inaction, as the motor for the barbaric behaviour of young men on council estates. Back towards what, in the late 1990s, passes as the political centre, the journalist and social commentator Melanie Phillips traces problems of crime and social disorder to the introduction of 'progressive' educational methods and the simultaneous emergence of moral relativism. She urges teachers to return to traditional classroom techniques and parents to specify clear moral values which accord with those of the right-thinking majority and to be unequivocal in their condemnation of moral laxity.

   Whatever else may divide them, most of these pundits are agreed upon the need for more state control over the bad behaviour of the young and their feckless fathers, and less state support for their welfare-dependent mothers. These ideas find their most coherent expression in the highly influential version of 'communitarianism' offered by Etzioni (1994), a doctrine which has been embraced by Tony Blair and Jack Straw. Etzioni writes: 'Communitarians call to restore civic virtues, for people to live up to their responsibilities and not merely focus on their entitlements, and to shore up the moral foundations of society.' He speaks of a pressing need to address the collapse of a common moral base and to inject a moral dimension into the task of social reconstruction. For Etzioni, the public humiliation of wrongdoers, 'naming and shaming', serves 'to underscore society's disapproval of the crime committed . . . Temporarily marking out those convicted in open court, after due process, seems a legitimate community-building device' (1994, p. 141). Etzioni indicates that the community must act as 'a reinforcer of pro-social mores' and in this there is little room for tolerance of minor infringements of rules, laws or norms and minor acts of public disorder.

This is a view of the world which finds many resonances in the 1997 Labour manifesto, which notes that 'the Conservatives have forgotten the "order" part of "law and order"'. In a similar vein, Jack Straw observed in a recent TV interview that 'The Prime Minister and I have spoken often about "zero tolerance policing". Some people, I know, do not like the label. I don't care about the terminology. I care about what works.' The provision in the Crime and Disorder Act (1998) for the imposition of child curfews for wandering 10-year-olds and a parenting order which may require their parents to engage in parenting and family education classes also aims to inculcate a sense of responsibility and an appropriate moral sensibility in those who are failing to meet their obligations to the community.

Not least of the problems occasioned by the uncritical ingestion of this new US-style electoral strategy and social philosophy is that ministers have come to imagine that we really are facing an American-style crime problem. Thus Jack Straw fulminates against 'aggressive beggars', human windscreen wipers and unaccompanied 10-year-olds hanging around Kentish Town High Street after dark as if he was talking about Chicago's South Side Ghetto, where firearms-related homicides, rather than mumbled requests for 'spare change', are an everyday reality.

Hard labour: the youth justice provisions of the Crime and Disorder Act

Ultimately New Labour's analysis of the problem of youth crime reduces it to a by-product of the moral failure of families, the cupidity of young offenders and the stupidity or incompetence of the professionals who are supposed to contain and educate them. In an attempt to correct this situation, New Labour has devised a youth justice strategy predicated upon partial 'dejuvenilisation' and a four-pronged strategy of pre-emptive intervention, prevention, incarceration and participation.

The erosion of the juvenile jurisdiction

The 'dejuvenilisation' of youth justice is, in part, a response to anxieties which surfaced in the early 1990s about 'a new breed of under age criminal whom the law cannot touch' (Hagell and Newburn, 1994; Pitts, 1995) epitomised by the eponymous 'ratboy', and Jon Venables and Robert Thompson, the two 10-year-olds who murdered two-year-old James Bulger in 1992. However the American influence on New Labour's youth justice strategy is also clearly evident in the Home Secretary's decision to abandon the principle of *doli incapax*. This principle does not imply, as Mr Straw seems to believe, that young people aged 10–13 are incapable of differentiating between right and wrong but, rather, that they *may* be incapable of differentiating between right and wrong, or understanding fully the consequences of their actions, by dint of their immaturity. This being so, the onus is therefore upon the prosecution to demonstrate criminal intent. As recently as 1990, in its White Paper, *Crime, Justice and Protecting the Public* (Home Office, 1990) the Conservative government noted that the principle of *doli incapax* should be retained because it made proper allowance for the fact that children's understanding, knowledge and ability to reason are still developing.

The other key principle which has informed juvenile and youth courts in the UK from their inception has been that the identity of defendants will not be revealed to the press or the public. The Home Secretary now has the discretion to give the courts the power to 'name and shame' young offenders. The Crime and Disorder Act also allows curfews, enforced by electronic tagging, to be extended to children and young people of 10 years and over, even though this measure will not be supervised by a member of the new Youth Offending Teams.

However the lowering to 12, or to 10 if the Home Secretary deems it politic, of the age at which youngsters can be sentenced to custodial confinement, in a secure training centre as subjects of a detention and training order, and the impending transfer of 18-year-olds back into the adult courts, constitute the radical edge of the government's dejuvenilising thrust.

Will it work?

In the USA since 1978, nearly all states have passed laws which restrict the jurisdiction of the juvenile courts and reallocate specified groups of offences and offenders to adult criminal jurisdictions (Feld, 1987; Szymanski, 1987; Wilson, 1994). These changes have been justified on the basis that juvenile courts offer neither adequate retribution for serious crimes committed by juveniles nor effective deterrence of subsequent crime (Feld, 1993; Wilson, 1983; Wolfgang, 1982). Proponents of 'dejuvenilisation' contend that adult criminal courts offer greater community protection (via incarceration in secure facilities) and more effective deterrence and proportionality between the offence and the penalty. However, as is indicated by Jeffrey Fagan's (1991) definitive study, which compared two cohorts of 200 juvenile offenders, matched in terms of the seriousness of their offences and their antecedents, who passed through juvenile courts in New Jersey and the adult criminal courts in New York, the 'going rate' for any given offence by young people with similar antecedents was similar in both jurisdictions and the deterrent effect was also identical. In fact, as was the case in an equivalent British study undertaken by the Home Office in 1983, if anything, the adult criminal court tended to err on the side of leniency. Consequently, the findings constitute a significant 'own goal' for the proponents of dejuvenilisation.

But even if the US research supported the case for the erosion of a separate juvenile jurisdiction, in attempting to make sense of youth justice policy in Britain we are still left with the difficulty that the USA presents problems of juvenile crime which, in terms of both their nature and their volume are, mercifully, profoundly different from the problems of youth crime in Britain. William Bratton, the erstwhile New York Police Chief, whose name is associated with the idea of 'zero tolerance' policing, recently observed on a visit to the UK that, with a youth murder rate 52 times lower than Washington, DC, Britain does not appear to have a youth crime problem worth worrying about. Yet Bratton, and his alleged methods, is routinely invoked by Jack Straw and certain 'gung ho' British police chiefs as the author of the solution to the problem of youth crime in Britain. As a commentator recently observed, turning to America to find a solution to the problem of UK youth crime is a bit like visiting Saudi Arabia to learn about women's rights.

It is, therefore, difficult to divine what, practically, these new Americanised measures, which almost certainly violate the UN Convention on the Rights of the Child, will achieve. Presumably, by eroding the distinctiveness of the youth justice system and bringing its protocols and penalties into line with the adult justice system, Mr Straw hopes he will appear to be 'hanging tough' in Worcester or wherever it is that the New Labour spin doctors believe the key to a second term is to be found.

Pre-emptive intervention

New Labour has adopted the view that crime and 'incivilities' are causally related and that, in order to reduce the former, an assault

---

The Crime and Disorder Act (1998)

Pre-emptive Interventions

> *The Local Child Curfew*
> *Child Safety Order*
> *Parenting Order*
> *Anti-Social Behaviour Order*

Pre-Court Preventive Interventions

> *Reprimand (once only)*
> *Final Warning (once only)*

Non-Custodial Preventive Disposals

> *Fine*
> *Action Plan Order*
> *Reparation Order*
> *Supervision Order*
> *Probation Order*
> *Community Service Order*
> *Combination Order*

Incarceration

> *Detention and Training Order (Indeterminate)*

must be made upon the latter. This idea is articulated most clearly by Wilson and Kelling (1982) and it has taken the form of a local child curfew, a child safety order and an anti-social behaviour order. The likely impact of these orders is discussed in Chapter 3.

These new pre-emptive measures extend the scope of the law significantly and are likely to encounter a succession of legal challenges if courts choose to impose them.

It is, of course, ironic that, whereas the community safety provisions of the 1998 Act aim to 'civilianise' crime control, the youth justice provisions strive to criminalise incivility.

Prevention

In 1995 the Audit Commission (1996) undertook a study of the operation of the youth justice system in England and Wales. It concluded that many of the resources committed to processing young offenders through the youth justice system could be better spent on the prevention of youth crime. It identified assistance with parenting skills, structured pre-school education for children at risk, support for teachers dealing with badly behaved pupils and the development of positive leisure opportunities for crime-prone children and young people as the keys to effective youth crime reduction. Rubbished upon its publication in 1996 by the Conservative government, the report, *Misspent Youth*, was welcomed by the Labour Party, which indicated that the recommendations of the report complemented its own youth justice strategy. Like the Morgan Report (Home Office, 1991) on community safety, which received a similarly frosty response from the Conservatives, *Misspent Youth* proposed that local authorities should assume statutory responsibility for developing multi-agency crime prevention initiatives.

The analysis of youth crime in *Misspent Youth* leans heavily upon certain explanations offered by developmental and cognitive–behavioural psychology and tends to play down the idea that if we are to make an impact on crime we might usefully attempt to change the social and economic circumstances of young offenders. The appeal of this approach to the problem for New Labour is fairly clear. At a time when politicians are unwilling to countenance social solutions to social problems, and eager to demonstrate that they are 'tough on the causes of crime', an analysis which identifies a lack of self-control as the fundamental problem, and a strategy which addresses the child-rearing practices of young lone parents and the class control techniques of young school teachers, must be hard to resist.

The renaissance of an individualised model of prevention will undoubtedly usher in a period of rapid expansion, and a central place in the new corporate community safety strategies, for statutory and voluntary youth justice and crime prevention agencies. For youth justice and crime prevention professionals, the renaissance of 'prevention' as a legitimate area of professional endeavour holds the promise that a broader repertoire of professional skills will be required of them than in the 1980s, when 'minimalism' reigned supreme.

Incarceration

The changes which are likely to have the greatest impact upon the numbers of children and young people who are sent into custody are the replacement of repeat cautioning by a once-and-for-all reprimand, followed by a final warning, the effective repeal of the conditional discharge and the downgrading of the supervision order from a 'direct alternative to custody' to a (pre-custodial) community penalty. The final warning will be given to a child or young person when they enter the youth justice system for the second time. Should they offend subsequently they will proceed directly to court. Until recently many police divisions in the UK operated a 'Caution Plus' programme which offered repeat offenders further cautions if they agreed to engage in programmes or undertake activities to which they were directed by the responsible police officer or youth justice worker. Home Office data indicate that approximately 15 per cent of young offenders entering the youth justice system in any year have received a previous caution. Many of these young people will now proceed directly to the youth court.

Conditional discharges have been the most frequently used disposals for male young offenders aged 10–13 in youth courts in England and Wales. Indeed, in the recent period they were increasingly popular with magistrates, growing from 39 per cent of all disposals in the age group in 1985 to 50 per cent in 1995. The Audit Commission has shown that they were also comparatively effective disposals, in that around 45 per cent of young people dealt with in this way did not reoffend and, of the remainder who did, around two-thirds offended less frequently. This compares with a 75 per cent plus reoffending rate for custodial sentences.

From 1998, most of the young offenders who are drawn into the youth court earlier in their offending careers by the imposition of a final warning will be denied the option of a conditional discharge and will, instead, be confronted by a fine, a community penalty or immediate custody. This will occur in a climate in which youth court sentencing is becoming harsher and the number of times community penalties may be offered is being restricted. This is likely to accelerate their progress towards custody.

Although Jack Straw has abandoned Michael Howard's ill-starred 'boot camps', five new secure training centres for the custodial confinement of children of 12 and over under the new detention and training order will be provided. This brings us perilously close to a 'three strikes and out' policy for children and young people in trouble.

In late 1998, Norman Warner, the newly appointed chair of the Youth Justice Board of England and Wales, agreed, when asked at a public seminar, that in the short term the use of custody for children and young people under the Crime and Disorder Act (1998) would continue to rise (recent Home Office data indicate that it has risen from about 1500 in young offender institutions (YOIs) at the end of the 1980s to 6200 in 1997). However, Norman Warner's answer to the question of what will happen in the longer term appears to be that we shall have to 'wait and see'.

Successive reports of the Chief Inspector of Prisons point to the inadequacies of YOI regimes and the unacceptable levels of violence, intimidation, drug abuse and suicide. Indeed child care specialists have observed that, were the 1989 Children Act applicable to prison department YOIs, most of the inmates would be on the child protection register simply by dint of residence there. Nonetheless the Crime and Disorder Act 1998 gives a central place to custodial penalties.

The final straw

Between 1989 and 1997 the number of juveniles, aged 15–18, held in Prison Department young offender institutions rose from 1400 to

6200. Asked how he planned to respond to the growing prison population, the Home Secretary, Jack Straw, answered that prisons were a 'demand-led service' and that if the bench chose to impose custodial sentences it was his job to provide the cells.

Participation

The fourth prong of New Labour's youth justice strategy is its education, training and welfare to work initiatives which aim to offer young people who would otherwise be excluded from participation in economic life and the education system a 'stake in conformity'. This marks an acceptance, albeit a somewhat grudging one, of a link between unemployment and crime and indicates a belief that education and employment will offer such a stake. There is considerable evidence that secure, reasonably paid, superannuated employment acts as a bulwark against crime. However, McGahey (1986) identifies a 'dual economy' in urban centres in which the labour market is divided into primary and secondary sectors. The primary sector labour market is characterised by steady jobs with reasonable wages and prospects for advancement. Workers in this sector tend to be older, better qualified, more reliable and better motivated, but these are qualities which are strengthened and reinforced by the higher quality and the greater stability of their jobs. The secondary sector labour market, by contrast, is characterised by low wage, sporadic, dead-end jobs which attract younger, less skilled, less well educated and less reliable employees. Like primary sector employment, the characteristics of the workforce are shaped by, and mirror, their conditions of employment. Residents in poor, high crime, neighbourhoods tend to derive their livelihood from a variety of sources: government transfers, employment and training programmes, crime and illegal hustles which, as McGahey (1986) has suggested, 'constitute important additional sources of income, social organisation and identity for the urban poor'. In low crime neighbourhoods, residents tend to derive their income, identity and sense of self-esteem from one, primary sector, employment source. The economic, demographic and policy changes of the 1980s were instrumental in eroding primary sector employment in the poorest neighbourhoods and, by default, promoting the development of secondary sector employment with its inevitable concomitant, the proliferation of illegitimate economic enterprises. This is a pattern the Labour strategy will have to change if it is to make a significant impact upon youth crime. If it does not work, and for those for whom it does not work, a tougher, less forgiving judicial and penal apparatus awaits.

2

Youth Crime in the UK

The rising crime rate

Between 1981 and 1993 recorded crime in the UK increased by 111 per cent. Government ministers were temporarily heartened in 1988 when it dropped by 5 per cent because it seemed that their investment in law and order, a real increase of 87 per cent during the Conservatives' period in office, was at last paying off. But recorded crime rose sharply again from the end of 1989, climbing by 17 per cent in 1990, a further 16 per cent in 1991, reaching its peak at 5.8 million in 1992, from where it fell back to around 5.3 million in 1994. However, the falls in recorded property crime between 1993 and 1994 were paralleled by a significant rise in 'crimes against the person' (see Table 2.1).

Violent crime in England and Wales

In England and Wales in 1994 the police recorded 312 000 violent crimes which constituted 6 per cent of all recorded offences. The figures for 1994 marked a 6.9 per cent increase on the previous year. Whether this represents a real increase in violence or, for example, simply tells us that the rapid spread of city centre CCTV is yielding higher levels of convictions for violence is unclear.

The incidence of youth offending

At first sight, there appears to be a serious discrepancy between data produced by the British Crime Survey (BCS), which asks householders about their victimisation, and Home Office criminal statis-

20

Table 2.1   Percentage changes in recorded crime, 1993–4

Vehicle crime	−9.6	Robbery	+3.3
Burglary	−8.2	Sexual offences	+3.9
Theft	−3.8	Violence against the person	+6.9

tics. The criminal statistics indicate that the numbers of young men aged 10–17 committing indictable offences in England and Wales fell by 38 per cent and the numbers of young women by 24 per cent between 1985 and 1995. Indeed, whereas between 11 per cent and 13 per cent of males born between 1953 and 1968 were *convicted* of at least one 'standard list' offence by the age of 17, only 6 per cent of males born in 1973 were thus convicted. These figures appear to show that today's 'teenagers' are less 'delinquent' than previous generations. Understandably, this 'fact' was seized upon by penal reformers as a vindication of the 'non-interventionist' delinquency management strategies of the 1980s and a reason why the more punitive youth justice policies introduced by Home Secretaries Kenneth Clarke, Michael Howard and Jack Straw should be resisted.

We should note, however, that the period saw a 25 per cent drop in the numbers of 10–17-year-olds in the population of England and Wales, increased informality in the treatment of 10–14-year-olds by the police, rigorous 'systems management' by youth justice professionals, an overall fall in the police clear-up rate and a fall in the court conviction rates.

In its 1992 enquiry into persistent young offenders, the House of Commons Home Affairs Select Committee was told by the Association of Chief Police Officers that recorded offences committed by children and young people had risen by 54 per cent (Hagell and Newburn, 1994). These 'facts' were, in turn, seized upon by some senior police officers, sections of the media and politicians across the board, as proof of the existence of a 'small hard core of very young offenders with absolutely no fears whatsoever of the criminal justice system'.

However, the data suggesting that a smaller number of offenders were committing a larger number of offences, taken together with BCS data on the distribution of crime and victimisation, suggested that the overall increase in recorded crime had been accompanied by changes in both its nature and geographical distribution (Hope, 1994).

The nature of youth offending

In 1992 the Home Affairs Select Committee had also called for a comprehensive Home Office study of offending by young people. In 1995 the study was published under the title *Young People and Crime* (Graham and Bowling, 1995). *Young People and Crime* aimed to identify why young people became involved in crime and why they stopped.

The study was based on interviews with young people aged between 14 and 25, undertaken in late 1992 and early 1993 by MORI. Of the young people interviewed, 893 were selected randomly from the population of England and Wales. A further 828 were selected from high-crime neighbourhoods and augmented by an 'ethnic minority booster sample' of 808 young people living mainly in inner city neighbourhoods. The young people were asked about their family life, their school experiences and their involvement with crime and drugs. Those who admitted offending were asked about how they started offending and, if they had stopped offending, why they had done so. The data were then subjected to a complex, multivariate, statistical analysis to establish key factors in the *onset* of and *desistance* from youth crime. In the second phase of the study, the researchers compiled 'life histories' of 21 'desisters', people who admitted committing three offences, or one serious offence, in the past, but not in the preceding year.

Offending careers

Contrary to the previously accepted wisdom amongst criminologists and youth justice professionals, the study appeared to show that young men involved in persistent offending tended not to 'grow out of crime' (Rutherford, 1986). Indeed it appears that, for some young men, offending continues, and sometimes intensifies, between the ages of 14 and 25. In this period, the types of crimes they commit change, with vandalism and other expressive crime giving way to property offences and violence, which then tail off in favour of fraud and theft from the workplace. This intensification of offending by young men in their 20s is often accompanied by much heavier drinking and drug-taking.

The study also indicates that some young people are persisting in what is, essentially, youth crime, long after adolescence. This suggests that youth, or adolescence, is not simply a question of chronology, but describes a period of transition. But, as Hagan (1993) has suggested, how long it lasts depends upon whether a young person has the social and economic wherewithal to proceed to the next stage in the life cycle.

In his study, undertaken in the USA during the great depression, W.F. Whyte (1943) 'hung out' with a group of 'corner boys' in an Italian neighbourhood. As the book proceeds, however, we realise that Doc and the Nortons are not teenagers but men, some of them in their mid to late 20s, and that they have been hanging out on the same corner for over 10 years. They have been doing this because, having no steady jobs, they have no money to pay rent, buy furniture and do all the other things one would need to do to become a 'family man' in Cornerville. They are, as a result, frozen in a state of perpetual youth or adolescence.

There is increasing evidence, both anecdotal and research-based (Hagan, 1993; Hope, 1994; Graham and Bowling, 1995), that a similar phenomenon is occurring in Britain in the 1990s, with the upper age of members of adolescent peer groups rising, in some instances, to over 30. Like Doc and the Nortons, these young people are unable to make the transition from adolescence to other higher status adult roles because they simply do not have the means to do so.

David Brindle writes:

Fewer that one in eight offenders serving probation is in full-time work or training, a survey by NAPO suggests today ... The survey was conducted in May among 1,331 offenders on probation in 19 areas of England and Wales. It found that 12 per cent had a full-time job or training place, with another 4 per cent receiving a mixture of income and benefits ... More than 30 of the 75 probation officers in the survey reported that over 90 per cent of their clients were dependent upon benefits ... People on probation are twice as likely as other jobless to be long-term unemployed. ('No-work plight for probationers', *The Guardian*, 16 August 1993)

Enforced adolescence means that young people on the social and economic margins are, quite literally, prevented from growing up. This has important implications for their involvement in crime because the evidence suggests that 'growing up', the assumption of adult roles, rights and responsibilities, also means growing out of crime (Rutherford, 1986).

The involvement of young women in crime reacher its peak at 16 and then falls off fairly sharply. Between the ages of 14 and 17 the level of involvement of young men and young women in crime is similar, 24 per cent and 19 per cent, respectively. However, by their early to mid-20s, 31 per cent of the young men surveyed were still involved in crime, whereas only 4 per cent of young women were. However, *Young People and Crime* reveals a much higher level of involvement of young women in crime than had previously been supposed. If the research is an accurate reflection of reality, it raises important questions about the under-representation of young women in the youth justice system.

White and Black British and Afro-Caribbean respondents reported similar levels of involvement in both crime in general and serious crime, yet research points to a significant overrepresentation of Black British and Afro-Caribbean people caught up in the youth and adult justice systems (Pitts, 1988; Krisburg and Austin, 1993). By 1992 10.8 per cent of male and 20.1 per cent of female prisoners in UK jails were Black British and Afro-Caribbean, yet non-white men of all nationalities in the UK constitute only 1.9 per cent of the population. In the interests of justice we need to establish whether this apparent overrepresentation of Black young men and the under-representation of young women is a product of their differential treatment by the police, social workers, probation officers and magistrates.

Asian young people, with the exception of those of Indian origin, reported a lower level of involvement in crime, although Indians committed fewer serious offences. Drug use amongst White respondents was higher than for all other groups. Just 3 per cent of respondents were responsible for 25 per cent of all the crime reported in the study and 21 per cent of young men and 5 per cent of young women had at some time committed a 'serious offence'.

Desistance from offending

When young women desisted from crime they tended to do so abruptly, leaving school, leaving home, setting up an independent household, often with a partner, and sometimes having a child as well. *Young People and Crime* appears to regard teenage motherhood positively because of its association with desistance from crime. The authors attribute this to a growth in maturity born of caring for another person. However, an alternative view suggests that early motherhood leads to desistance from crime because it takes young women 'out of circulation'. It separates them from friends and family and often pushes them into hard-to-let flats in high-crime neighbourhoods. Here their chances of becoming victims of crime are greatly increased (Hope, 1994). This isolation and victimisation may in turn contribute to the disproportionate incidence of depression amongst these young women, and their consequent induction into a psychiatric, rather than a criminal, career. The new national standards for youth justice promulgated by the Inner London Youth Justice Service (ILYJS, 1995) suggest that we should now regard a young person in trouble as a young person in need. The plight of these young women offers us a vivid example of the reasons why some youth justice professionals are arguing that we might usefully shift from an often myopic focus upon the cost-effective management of local youth justice systems towards the construction of a more robust youth justice service which is committed to a genuine partnership with socially disadvantaged young people and the alleviation of the multiplicity of difficulties they face.

For young men, the major factors in desistance from crime were associated with not leaving home and continuing to live with parents which, in turn, allowed them to avoid the worst excesses of drink and drug abuse and too close an association with other young offenders. However, whether they were able to stay at home depended on the quality of the relationship they had with their parents.

The characteristics of young offenders

Young men and young women who offended persistently shared a number of characteristics. While the authors found no correlation with race, and only a weak correlation with social class and family size, family poverty and a family's capacity to supervise its children appeared to be associated with involvement in youth crime.

Young people living with both their natural parents were less likely to offend than those in one-parent families or living with a step-parent. Poor relationships with step-parents correlated closely with persistent involvement in crime. Young people who reported being less attached to their families were more likely to be involved in crime and those who ran away from home before they were 16 were particularly likely to offend, as were males who had a poor relationship with their fathers. Young people whose brothers and sisters had been in trouble with the law were more likely to get into trouble themselves. Involvement with friends who were involved in crime emerged as one of the most powerful factors in a young person's involvement or persistence in crime. Truancy, school exclusion, poor academic attainment and a belief that they were an 'academic failure' were also closely related to a young person's sustained involvement in crime. Over 80 per cent of the young men and 60 per cent of the young women who were persistently involved in crime shared four or five of these characteristics.

Crime and neighbourhood change

Because of the way the research was conducted, *Young People and Crime* does not tell us about the geographical distribution of youth crime. However, roughly two-thirds of the data in the study were gathered in high-crime and inner-city neighbourhoods and it could be that the factors identified by the research as being associated with onset and desistance are, in fact, a product of a 'neighbourhood effect' rather than randomly distributed problems of families and schools. Were this to be the case, it would echo much recent research in the UK and the USA which suggests that since the late 1970s youth crime and many other social problems have become progressively concentrated in neighbourhoods with a preponderance of poor, young families, rapid population change and weakening, sometimes non-existent, links with the local economy. These are the neighbourhoods in which young people fail to grow out of crime and where, as a result, persistent and serious youth crime becomes embedded.

An analysis of British Crime Survey data for the decade 1982 to 1992 reveals an alarming picture. The survey divided neighbourhoods into 10 categories on the basis of the intensity of the criminal victimisation of their residents. By 1992, the chances of a resident in the lowest crime neighbourhood ever being assaulted had fallen to a point where it was barely measurable. Residents in the highest crime neighbourhoods, by contrast, now risked being assaulted twice a year. This polarisation of risk is made clearer when we recognise that by 1992, residents in the highest crime neighbourhoods experienced twice the rate of property crime and four times the rate of personal crime of those in the next worst category. These findings point to a dramatic redistribution of victimisation towards the poorest and most vulnerable residents over the intervening decade Hope (1994).

As the 1980s progressed, a combination of the government's 'right to buy' policy, 'Tenant Incentive Schemes' which offered more prosperous council tenants a contribution towards their mortgages if they moved into private sector housing, the curtailment of the right of local authorities to spend housing revenue on housebuilding, and progressive reductions in central government's financial contribution to local government ensured that less and less public housing stock was available for rent. These developments presaged significant demographic changes in which relatively prosperous elderly and higher income families left housing estates in the inner city or on its periphery, to be replaced by poorer, younger families (Page, 1993). As a result, whereas at the beginning of the 1980s the average council house tenant's income was 73 per cent of the national average, by the beginning of the 1990s it had fallen to 48 per cent. By 1995, over 50 per cent of council households had no breadwinner (Rowntree, 1996). The estates which experienced the greatest changes saw increasing concentrations of children, teenagers, young single adults and young single parent families. These neighbourhoods also became a last resort for residents who had previously been homeless, hospitalised or imprisoned, and for refugees from political persecution.

These rapid demographic changes quickly eroded relationships of kinship and friendship, transforming these estates into aggregates of strangers, who were often deeply suspicious of one another. This had a number of consequences. It meant that those people most vulnerable to criminal victimisation, young single parents, Black and

Asian families and the single elderly, and those most likely to vic-
timise them, adolescent boys and young men, were progressively
thrown together on the poorest housing estates. In their study of one
such neighbourhood in the early 1990s, Tim Hope and Janet Foster
(1992) found that a 40 per cent turnover in population over three
years was paralleled by a 50 per cent rise in burglaries. However
rapid population change meant that traditional forms of informal
social control also disappeared. Alongside the disappearance of
informal systems of social control we also saw the erosion of traditional systems of informal social support for parents, young people
and children which often made the difference between whether a
child or young person could be sustained in a fragile or volatile home
situation or not. The American criminologist Elliott Currie writes:

> Communities suffering from these compounded stresses begin
> to exhibit the phenomenon some researchers call 'drain': as the
> ability of families to support themselves and care for their chil-
> dren drops below a certain critical point, they can no longer
> sustain those informal networks of social support and help that
> can otherwise be a buffer against the impact of the economic
> grinding of the market. (Currie, 1991, p. 346)

Because people were disconnected from one another, participation
in local political and social life was minimal and so people had no
basis upon which to join together to exert political pressure, bid for
resources and make demands on the local and central government
agencies with responsibility for the problems they confronted.

Since 1990, Robert Sampson *et al.* (1997) have been investigating
whether, or to what extent, neighbourhood crime rates are a function of that neighbourhood's social and organisational characteristics, rather than the characteristics of the individuals and families
who live there. This research has involved 8782 residents in 343
Chicago neighbourhoods. Sampson concludes:

> Past research has consistently reported links between neighbour-
> hood social composition and crime. In the current study, the
> researchers found that in neighbourhoods scoring high on collec-
> tive efficacy (social cohesion and trust), crime rates were 40 per
> cent below those in low scoring neighbourhoods. This difference

supported the researchers' basic premise – crime rates are not solely attributable to individuals' aggregate demographic characteristics. Rather, crime is a function of neighbourhood social and organisational characteristics.

High crime neighbourhoods tend to be highly concentrated and have a distinctive economic structure. In Britain in the 1980s, neighbourhood destabilisation, by eroding economic links between poor neighbourhoods and their local economies, reproduced this structure in growing numbers of poor neighbourhoods. In the process inner city retail, industrial and commercial concerns, which had once been central to the social and demographic stability of working class neighbourhoods, either went out of business or relocated in the industrial and retail parks on the periphery of the city. The impact of this mass evacuation was compounded by a policy shift in the mid-1980s which meant that training resources followed employers rather than 'job-seekers'.

The Vera study, undertaken in New York in the 1980s, showed that the key factor determining the level and nature of crime in working class neighbourhoods was adult involvement in primary sector employment. The study found that the quality and quantity of jobs in a neighbourhood determined the ways people formed households, regulated their own behaviour, and the public behaviour of others and used public services. The resulting neighbourhood atmosphere then helped to shape the incentives for residents to engage in legitimate employment or income-oriented crime. A high level of adult involvement in primary sector employment produced stable households, stable families, stable social relationships and enhanced vocational opportunities for the next generation. A low level of involvement had the opposite effect. This study also revealed that, in the first instance, the factors determining a neighbourhood's crime rate and its capacity to contain crime were almost all visited upon it from the outside in the form of social and economic policies, economic fluctuations, the drugs trade, demographic destabilisation and benefit levels.

In their study entitled *Individual Risk Factors, Neighbourhood Socio-Economic Status (SES) and Youth Offending*, Wikstrom and Loeber (1997) found that, in neighbourhoods with relatively high socioeconomic status (SES), certain personal risk factors (hyperactivity–impulsivity, attention deficit, poor parental monitoring, poor school motivation, positive attitudes towards delinquency, and lack of guilt) correlated positively with involvement in crime. However, in neighbourhoods with low SES, serious offending by young people with low individual risk factors was far more prevalent. They also discovered that young people with no risk factors appeared to be most seriously affected by low neighbourhood SES, and that low neighbourhood SES was a far more reliable predictor of youth criminality in these neighbourhoods than individual risk factors.

A youth crime implosion

The bulk of the crime and violence in these neighbourhoods is committed by local children and young people and is often directed against other local children and young people, in and out of school. These are the neighbourhoods where racially motivated violence and gang fighting is most prevalent. In a period of economic boom, the young people in these neighbourhoods would have cut their ties with the school and the neighbourhood and got on with adult life. Now, people of 18 and older are condemned to seek such status as they can from a peer group whose members may be as young as 12. Thus they are only semi-detached from the neighbourhood and the school, its social networks and its tensions, and conflicts which begin in the school can spill over into the neighbourhood where they attract older unemployed teenagers and young adults. Similarly conflicts which begin in the neighbourhood may sometimes be fought out in the school. We are therefore confronted once again by the paradox of economic globalisation, paralleled by the development of local tribalism. Condemned to a 'ghettoised' form of life, these young people were progressively cut off from active participation in the sociocultural and economic mainstream, with only the school to offer them a way out.

  These are also the neighbourhoods in which racist attacks, small-scale riots and drug-related crime and violence proliferated in the 1980s (Pearson, 1987; Lea and Young, 1988; Campbell, 1993). Geoffrey Pearson observes that:

> even within a town or a city with a major [drugs] problem it will tend to be concentrated in certain neighbourhoods and virtually

unknown in others. Moreover, where the problem has tended to gather together in dense pockets within our towns and cities, this will usually be in neighbourhoods which are worst affected by unemployment and wretched housing. (Pearson, 1987, pp. 190–1)

Not surprisingly, perhaps, these are also the neighbourhoods from which the bulk of the children in care, or being 'looked after' by the local authority, are drawn and where the preponderance of young people who run away, and stay away, from home originate (Currie, 1991; Pitts, 1997). An analysis of data supplied by the homelessness charity Centrepoint reveals that, overwhelmingly, young people who run away from, or are thrown out of, home come from regions with the highest levels of unemployment in general, and youth unemployment in particular. Many of them have spent some time in care. Many report that they leave home as a result of conflict with parents, and this conflict often concerns money, or its absence. An analysis of the data for London reveals that over 70 per cent of the runaways who reached Centrepoint came from the poorest Inner London boroughs. A study undertaken in Luton revealed that 46 per cent of the young people who ran away from home came from the poorest public housing estate with the highest crime rate, lowest level of youth employment and political participation in the borough.

But while it is possible to produce evidence to support a link between economic and political change, neighbourhood destabilisation and running away, surely abuse is of a different order altogether? Well, yes and no! Most people today would accept that child abuse, in the forms of sexual violation and violence, is, for the most part, perpetrated by men and that it occurs throughout the social structure. However, recent scholarship (Messerschmidt, 1993; Segal, 1990; Campbell, 1993) suggests that, rather than being randomly distributed, crimes against women and children tend to be concentrated in the poorest neighbourhoods. As we have seen, Currie attributes this, in part at least, to the progressive drain upon parenting capacities which life in destabilised neighbourhoods imposes. In addition, however, we should note that this violence is most prevalent amongst men who experience the greatest discrepancy between what they have become and what they believe, as men, they are supposed to be. If, as many commentators argue, the violent sexual abuse of women and children is essentially about power rather than sex, it should not surprise us that it is concentrated in what Lynne Segal (1990) describes as 'the underclass'. This begins to explain the prevalence of child abuse and domestic violence in destabilised neighbourhoods. In response to these developments Currie (1991) has advocated 'a wide range of supports for parents in coping with real world stresses in their communities'; however, the political changes of the 1980s and 1990s have served only to erode these services.

The decline of public services

The plight of the families in these neighbourhoods has been compounded by cutbacks in local government expenditure which have resulted in the withdrawal of many of the educational, youth service, community development and social welfare services which had previously contributed to the quality of communal life and social cohesion in their neighbourhoods. However, it is not simply that there was greater need and fewer organisations and individuals available to respond to that need. In the 1980s, the nature of both public services and 'publics' themselves changed. The 1980s witnessed swingeing cuts in local authority budgets, a substantial redistribution of political power from local to central government and the parallel introduction of 'market forces' into public services (Hutton, 1995). In this period, decisions about the goals to which public services should strive, their spending priorities and the day-to-day conduct of their staff were increasingly taken by central government or the government's appointees in the burgeoning, and largely unaccountable, 'QuANGOcracy' which progressively annexed public services in the 1980s. Together, these forces have seriously restricted the capacity of local agencies to make a concerted collaborative response to the profound problems experienced by the residents of destabilised neighbourhoods.

Conclusion

In *Young People and Crime*, Graham and Bowling (1995) suggest a three-tier approach to prevention comprising universal services, additional neighbourhood services in high crime areas and spe-cialised services, which focus upon families whose children are per-sistently involved in crime and upon the schools they attend. This strategy is, of course, reminiscent of the welfarist initiatives of the 1960s and 1970s. However, as we have noted, it is evident that structural weaknesses within neighbourhood social and economic structures will overwhelm the best efforts of even the most enlight-ened and adequately resourced service providers. Although, like the Audit Commission report *Misspent Youth* (1996), Graham and Bowling's policy recommendations emphasise interventions to strengthen families and schools and the relationship between them, their research reveals that only one in 10 of the 16–17-year-old 'persisters' interviewed was in stable full-time employment and that even by their mid-20s only half of the men and one-third of the women had a 'steady job'. This remarkable finding receives little attention in the recommendations, a fact which is probably attrib-utable to the Conservative government's unwillingness to make, or allow to be made, any causal connection between crime and unem-ployment. It is nonetheless clear, as McGahey (1986) and Sullivan (1989) have demonstrated, that exclusion from the legitimate labour market was a highly significant factor in young people's persistence in crime.

This being the case, it would seem reasonable to suggests that local youth justice and community safety initiatives which aim to reduce crime need to be rooted in a local analysis of crime and desis-tance, demographic change and the participation of residents in the local and regional economies. Thus, strategies developed by workers in youth justice and community safety would need to articulate with initiatives by local government directorates and central government departments which aim to rebuild local economies and stabilise the populations of high-crime, high-social need neighbourhoods. This is the context in which the bald 'facts' of the relationship between youth crime, the family and the school take on meaning. However, as we have already noted, we live in a time in which social solutions to social problems are deeply unpopular. It is much easier to talk of the need to inject a new sense of responsibility into lax parents and a new discipline into the education of the young than to confront what is happening in our cities and the run-down housing estates on their periphery. The tedious rhetoric of 'individual responsibility' belies a stark reality in which growing numbers of young people are being driven to desperate, often self-destructive, lengths in order to salvage a livelihood and a plausible identity from an increasingly barren social and economic environment.

3

The Youth Justice System: from Arrest to Prosecution

The term 'youth justice system', when it is used in this book, refers to the laws, professional practices and institutions created to respond to children and young people aged between 10 and 18 years in England and Wales (8 and 18 years in Scotland) who are suspected of committing, or found guilty of, a criminal offence.

Local youth justice systems

It would be wrong to assume that the youth justice system in England and Wales, or in Scotland, is a national institution which dispenses justice uniformly throughout the land. The youth justice system is, in fact, composed of a multiplicity of local youth justice systems which are characterised by diversity rather than uniformity. Indeed, in some cases, what happens to a child or young person caught up in the youth justice system may be determined more by the area in which he or she commits an offence than by its seriousness. It is for this reason that in the 1980s and 1990s both the Home Office and the Association of Directors of Social Services developed national standards for adult and youth justice.

These differences between local youth justice systems are determined in large part by the formal and informal relationships which are established between the agencies and agents which constitute the system, and the ways in which they choose to use their powers. Systems are characterised by interdependence; each agent or agency within the system needs the others and so, in varying degrees, power is bestowed upon them all. Capra (1982) notes that systems are characterised by 'the inter-relatedness and interdependence of all phenomena', observing that 'an integrated whole whose properties cannot be reduced to those of its parts is called a system'. A systemic perspective alerts us to the reality that, when agents and agencies within a system effect choices about whether, and how, to use their power, those choices will have consequences for the whole system. They will affect the youngster's life in significant ways and it follows that, if we are to work in the interests of the young offender, it will often be these relationships and these choices which will constitute the target for our interventions and the exercise of our power. Systems can be sites of conflict, consensus or negotiation. What they become will be determined by the ways in which the actors within them choose to use their power.

A new framework for youth justice

In November 1997, the Government published the White Paper *No More Excuses*, in which it outlined its strategy for tackling youth crime (Home Office, 1997). The White Paper's recommendations were translated into law in the Crime and Disorder Act (Home Office, 1998) which makes important changes to the youth justice system and places new statutory responsibilities upon the police and local authorities to devise community safety strategies, and to prevent crime and criminality. Some of the changes introduced by the Act concern penalties which can be imposed by youth courts while other *preventive* measures, like the local child curfew and the child safety order, are concerned with children and young people at risk of involvement in crime and are primarily aimed at agencies working outside the youth justice system.

The local child curfew

The Crime and Disorder Act (1998) states that 'for their own good, and to prevent neighbourhood crime or disorder, young children should not be out, unsupervised late at night'. In so saying, the Act provides new powers for local authorities and the police to set up an area curfew which will prohibit children under 10 from being in specified public places unless supervised by a responsible adult between certain specified times (such as 9.00 pm to 6.00 am). Before establishing a scheme, a local authority must consult the police and the 'local community', and obtain approval from the Home Secretary. Local child curfews established under an approved scheme may only last for up to 90 days. If the local authority seeks an extension beyond this time, it must again consult the police and local community.

A child under 10 who is found out unaccompanied in a curfew area during curfew hours may be taken home by the police and placed in the care of a responsible person. If there is no responsible person there to look after him or her, the police can use powers already available to them under sect. 46 of the Children Act (Department of Health, 1989) to remove the child to 'other suitable accommodation'. The White Paper notes that:

> Curfew schemes should provide an effective immediate method of dealing with clearly identified problems of anti-social and disorderly children who are too young to be left out unsupervised late at night. Schemes should be integrated into the area's wider community-safety strategy.

The rationale for the local child curfew is primarily political and it will inevitably bear upon the most socially disadvantaged neighbourhoods and the most overcrowded families. In a previous era, the objectives the order aims to achieve were secured via after-school activities, play centres, youth projects and neighbourhood adventure playgrounds. The order may well prove costly, time-consuming and ineffective, since it is almost certain that the old game of 'being a bloody nuisance' will, forthwith, be augmented by the new one of 'curfew hopping'. A breach of the local child curfew provides grounds for the imposition of further orders (the child safety order and the parenting order), breaches of which may, in turn, trigger care proceedings in the family proceedings court. Thus the local child curfew promises to become a 'fast-track' to care and custody in its own right. This is yet another reason why the police and the local authorities are unlikely to develop a great deal of enthusiasm for the order.

The child safety order

The child safety order is designed to 'protect' children under 10, the age of criminal responsibility (in England and Wales), who have already 'started to behave in an anti-social or criminal manner' or are deemed by the local authority to be in danger of becoming involved in crime. The order can only be used when the local authority can show that:

- the child has done something which would constitute an offence if he or she were over 10;
- the child's behaviour suggests that he or she is 'at risk' of offending;
- the child is disruptive or harassing other residents; or
- the child has breached a local curfew order.

The child safety order will be granted by the family proceedings court and not the youth court. Under this order a court may require a child to be home at a certain time or stay away from certain people or places, or to attend school. A child safety order can be linked with a parenting order if the court feels that this is appropriate. If the requirements of a child safety order are not complied with, the local authority may commence care proceedings under sect. 31(l) (*a*) of the Children Act (1989).

The most obvious objection to the child safety order is that it will serve to 'criminalise' children below the age of criminal responsibility even if the behaviour for which the order is imposed is not, in fact, criminal.

The anti-social behaviour order

An anti-social behaviour order may be sought by the police or the local authority from a civil court. The order can require the subject of the order to refrain from certain behaviours or activities or not to enter certain places at certain times. Thus, for example, if a young person is suspected of loitering around schools at break times in order to sell drugs to the students, an anti-social behaviour order may require them not to come within 500 metres of the school between the hours of 8.00 am and 6.00 pm. This provision means that quasi-criminal penalties may be imposed without recourse to the judicial process and the rules of evidence.

Arrest and interrogation

Most young people enter the youth justice system when they are arrested by the police. In making that arrest the police are required to abide by the requirements of the Police and Criminal Evidence Act (1984) (PACE) and the subsequent Home Office Codes of Practice which specify the rights of 'juveniles', young people aged between 10 and 17 in England and Wales. Perhaps the most important of these rights is the requirement that an 'appropriate adult' be present when a young person is informed of their rights, interviewed about an alleged offence and searched or placed in an identification parade. Under PACE the police are required to contact a parent, guardian or carer or, failing that, another person responsible for the youngster's welfare, as soon as practicable after the arrest. Normally the child's parent, guardian or carer would undertake the role of appropriate adult, but in cases where this is not possible, because they are unavailable or uncooperative, this service will be provided by *youth offending teams*.

The role of the appropriate adult is to safeguard the young person's rights, interests and welfare and to minimise the risk of interviews generating unreliable and detrimental evidence. All children and young people who have been arrested have a right to free legal advice, although only about 25 per cent of arrested juveniles take advantage of this option. One of the key roles of the appropriate adult is, therefore, to ensure that the young person has adequate legal representation.

From cautions to final warnings

The 1997 *No More Excuses* White Paper indicates that 'the great majority of young offenders commit offences only once or twice. In these cases, a warning by the police is often the most effective way of preventing further crime'. Citing evidence from *Misspent Youth* that around 68 per cent of offenders who are cautioned for the first time are neither cautioned again nor reconvicted within two years, the White Paper notes that, in terms of reconviction, cautions grow progressively less effective as they are repeated. It notes that the trouble with the 'current cautioning system' is that it is 'too haphazard'. Indeed, in England and Wales, three out of five apprehended young offenders are cautioned, although the proportion varies enormously from area to area. Whereas, for example, in 1986 the Northamptonshire police cautioned 85 per cent of the boys and 95 per cent of the girls it apprehended, the figures for Staffordshire were 43 per cent and 88 per cent, respectively. The White Paper also bemoaned the fact that 'too often a caution does not result in any follow up action and so the opportunity for early intervention is lost' and it concludes that 'inconsistent, repeated and ineffective cautioning has allowed some children and young people to feel that they can offend with impunity'.

In consequence, the Crime and Disorder Act (1998) abolishes cautioning for young offenders and replaces it with a statutory police *reprimand* and a *final warning*. It will then be for the police to decide whether to reprimand a young offender, give a final warning, or bring criminal charges. When a final warning is given, it will usually be followed by a community intervention programme, involving the offender, and his or her family, to address the causes of the offending and so reduce the risk of further crime. The Home Office consultation paper *Tackling Youth Crime* (1997) explains the final warning scheme thus:

- a first offence might be met by a police reprimand, provided it was not serious. Any further offence would have to result in a Final Warning or Criminal Charges: in no circumstances should a young offender receive two reprimands;
- if a first offence results in a Final Warning, any further offence would automatically lead to criminal charges, except where at least two years have passed since the Final Warning, and the subsequent offence is minor; and
- for any offence for which the police would have the option of pressing charges.

The government appears to be convinced that the final warning scheme will ensure that 'more consistent action is taken, before a young offender ever appears in court, to try to nip offending in the bud'. The White Paper notes that final warning interventions will build upon existing 'caution plus' schemes where they exist. These schemes characteristically include elements of restorative justice, a confrontation with offending behaviour, social skills workshops and sessions concerned with education, work, family and health.

Making decisions

When the final warning is in operation, following an initial interview, the police will decide whether there is sufficient evidence to prove that the young person committed the offence and, if so, whether they should issue a *reprimand*, a *final warning* or whether it is *in the public interest* to charge the child or young person and pass the case to the Crown Prosecution Service for *prosecution*. In making these decisions police forces have often used an index of 'gravity factors' (Table 3.1) which categorises offences by degrees of seriousness and identifies exacerbating and mitigating factors. It is likely that similar instruments will be used by youth offending teams when devising their recommendations.

Youth offending teams (YOTs)

The Home Office plans to establish YOTs between April 1999 and March 2000. Every local authority with education and social services responsibilities will be required to ensure that one or more YOTs are established in the area they serve. YOTs will be staffed by seconded personnel from the local authority, the police, the probation service, education and the health service. Each team will have a steering group made up of senior representatives of the agencies involved and these steering groups will link with:

- Drug Action Teams,
- Community Safety and Crime Reduction Partnerships,
- Area Child Protection Committees,
- Area Criminal Justice Liaison Committees, and
- Social and Economic Regeneration Groups.

While welcoming the advent of YOTs, the National Association for Youth Justice (NAYJ), the youth justice practitioners organisa-

Table 3.1   Gravity factor inventory

Offences	Gravity score	Offence-specific factors	
		+	−
Robbery	5	Possessed weapon	Used minimum threat
Grievous bodily harm	4	Used weapon	Provoked
Burglary	4	Night time Occupier present Deliberately frightened occupants	Vacant premises Coerced by others
Car theft	3	Premeditated	For own family
Theft	3	Planned Unrecovered property	Poverty
Handling	3	Property stolen to order	Under pressure
Criminal damage	3	Group offence Damage over £200	Impulsive Less than £50
Possession of drugs	3	In prison Large quantity	Bought by group to share
Common assault	2	Injury caused, premeditated	Impulsive action

General factors for all offences

+	−
Conviction likely to result in significant sentence	Small or nominal penalty likely
Offender in position of trust	Genuine mistake or misunderstanding
Offence committed while defendant on bail	Offender has put right harm or loss caused
Offender has previous conviction or caution for comparable offence	Influence by others more criminally sophisticated

Score	Action
5	Prosecute
4	Prosecute unless police decision maker can justify not doing so
3	Pivotal
2	High probability of caution
1	Warning

Source: Association of Chief Police Officers, cited in the Audit Commission Report, *Misspent Youth* (1996, p. 21).

tion, has expressed strong reservations about their name. It argues that the term 'youth offending teams' places too much emphasis upon 'young offenders', as opposed to young people who have committed offences. They believe that this could lead to the stigmatisation of the young people receiving the service. The association believes that they should be called 'youth development' or 'youth justice' teams.

YOTs will co-ordinate the provision of local youth justice services. They may provide these services directly or co-ordinate their provision by other statutory, voluntary or private sector agencies. The minimum services they will provide directly are:

- appropriate adult services;
- assessment and intervention work in support of final warnings administered by the police;
- bail information and support services;
- the placement of children and young people on transfer from the police, and on remand from the court, in open or secure accommodation, remand fostering or approved lodgings;
- the preparation of court reports;
- the co-ordination of provision of responsible officers for child safety orders and parenting orders and undertaking such supervision work (this will require close liaison with social services);
- the supervision of children and young people sentenced to an action plan order, reparation order, supervision order, probation order, community service order or combination order (this may include drawing on programmes and activities provided outside the youth offending team);
- through-care and post-release supervision for young people sentenced to a detention and training order or other custodial sentence.

A number of senior figures in the probation service have argued vociferously that they should be the lead agency in youth offender teams by dint of the experience and expertise within the service. However this overlooks the fact that the service has carried no responsibility for juveniles since 1964 and that, by the late 1990s, its stock in trade was the supervision of high-tariff adult offenders.

The ways in which YOTs will discharge their roles on the ground can be inferred from the inter-agency youth justice panels currently in operation, many of which operate 'caution plus' schemes of the type cited approvingly by the Audit Commission (1996) as a model for interventions which could accompany the final warning.

these [inter-agency panels] typically include representatives from the police, probation service, education, social services and education welfare. Occasionally others such as the youth service and community groups may be represented on the panel. Ideally the panel members work as a team and make joint decisions and recommendations to the police who hold final responsibility for decision-making. It should also be recognised and accepted that decision-making can be difficult. This is because the different agencies involved have different roles and different primary responsibilities in respect of young people. (NACRO, 1987, p.5)

Effective inter-agency work requires the active collaboration of the statutory and voluntary agencies involved and the police. It should be monitored and evaluated rigorously in order to keep it on track. For that reason, participants need to be committed to shared goals, shared methods of data collection and the development and modification of professional and administrative practices as the strategy develops over time. Much of the research on inter-agency collaboration in the sphere of crime prevention points to the fact that 'partnership' is not enough and that it is the development of shared experience and a shared 'culture' which determines the effectiveness of such partnerships. This research also suggests that the active support and commitment of key figures at the head of the participating agencies is essential if they are to be more than talking shops in which agencies simply attempt to discharge or displace their own agency responsibilities, or forums in which the most powerful agency attempts to co-opt the others in order that it can discharge its pre-existing role more effectively. However many inter-agency panels have surmounted these problems and the following mission statement of a panel in an inner city borough gives a flavour of their ethos.

The Walford Panel aims to prevent the continued involvement in crime of Walford children and young people aged between 10 and

17 who come to the attention of the police. The Panel aims to ensure that children and young people recognise the seriousness of their behaviour and its actual and potential consequences for themselves and their victims. Nonetheless, the panel will operate in accordance with the UN Convention on the Rights of the Child, the Children Act (1989) and the Protocol on Standards in Youth Justice issued by the Association of Directors of Social Services, which emphasise that the child or young person in trouble is also a 'child in need'. Thus the panel recognises that children and young people in trouble are growing and changing and that its work with them must have a 'developmental' orientation which promotes growth towards maturity and the development of high self esteem. It is therefore committed to responses to children and young people which build upon their strengths, rather than dwell upon their weaknesses, and strive to open up new opportunities for success rather than underlining past failures. Ultimately, the Panel is interested in what children and young people can become rather than what they have been in the past. As such, whenever and wherever possible, the panel will create interventions which are integrative rather than segregative, enabling young people to gain satisfaction from, and contribute creatively to, their homes, their schools and their neighbourhoods. The major administrative instrument whereby these goals are to be achieved will be the inter-agency panel.

Perhaps the best known, longest running, and certainly the best resourced, inter-agency panel is the one in Northamptonshire which manages the 'Northants Diversion Scheme', which is discussed in detail in Chapter 9.

The Crown Prosecution Service

Once charges have been made against a defendant the case is referred to the Crown Prosecution Service (CPS) The CPS is a central government body, which operates from regional offices. Its primary tasks are to evaluate evidence in order to decide whether there is a reasonable chance of a conviction being gained if a case is brought to court, to prosecute those cases in court and make recommendations to courts concerning the granting of bail. Crown prosecutors have discretion to discontinue a prosecution if it appears that it would not be in the public interest to proceed with it. Where such discretion is exercised it would normally be on the grounds that the offence is not a serious one or that the defendant is very young, or elderly and infirm. In some areas the probation service works with the CPS in making 'public interest case assessments' which provide the CPS with fuller information on a defendant's circumstances. The probation service may also provide the CPS with information concerning the granting of bail.

4

The Youth Justice System: the Youth Court

Youth courts (formerly known as juvenile courts) were introduced in England and Wales in October 1992. At this point the child care and protection responsibilities of the juvenile court were transferred to a new *family proceedings court*, brought into being by the Children Act (1989) to deal with non-criminal matters relating to children. These include care proceedings, adoption, child protection, residence and contact. All applications relating to these orders (except in cases of divorce) begin in this court, but may ultimately be dealt with by a higher court. Prior to October 1992, juvenile courts dealt with children and young people up to the age of 17. From this date onwards, however, their jurisdiction was extended to include 17-year-olds, thus bringing the age of the 'juvenile jurisdiction' into line with the age of majority in the UK. However, shortly after its election in 1997, the Labour government, wishing to appear 'tougher' than their Tory predecessors, announced that young offenders over 16 were, once again, to be dealt with by adult courts.

Youth courts tend to be less formal than the adult courts. The public are excluded and although the press are admitted to the court room, journalists may not report the names of the children or young people who appear before the court. However, Jack Straw, the Home Secretary, is keen to scrap this convention and allow the press to 'name and shame' some young offenders. In Italy, where there is no such constraint upon the press, naming and shaming of young offenders has led, in some cases, to violent reprisals against children in trouble and their families.

Youth court magistrates

The youth court is usually presided over by three lay magistrates, one of whom acts as chairperson. Sometimes, usually in large cities, a stipendiary magistrate who is a legally trained professional may hear cases alone.

The institution of the magistracy dates back to feudal times and was brought into being in an attempt to exert some control over drunkenness and crime amongst young people. The continuance of this ancient institution into the modern world is justified on the grounds that it offers an invaluable repository of lay common sense. It is argued that the attitudes, and beliefs of lay magistrates will be more akin to those of the 'man in the street' than those of lawyers and judges, recruited largely from the upper middle classes. It is said that a magistracy composed of people from different social backgrounds with differing views, attitudes and opinions will reflect the range of moral and social attitudes held in the wider society. Thus the magistracy is presented as an important democratising and humanising element in the justice system.

Research has cast doubt upon the extent to which magistrates *are* representative of the wider society. Despite some changes in the 1980s and 1990s, the social make-up of the bench remains slanted in favour of the propertied, prosperous, well-educated and white, while the defendants tend to be propertyless, poor, badly-educated and disproportionately black. The diversity of views held by magistrates may make them representative as a body but will tend to make them unrepresentative as individuals and it is as individuals that they hear cases. Thus, as we have noted, penalties imposed upon both adults and juveniles can vary significantly from court to court, and from area to area, reflecting the idiosyncrasies of particular courts or individual magistrates rather than what the public might feel is just (Burney, 1979; King and May, 1985; Parker *et al.*, 1989).

Justice by geography

These idiosyncrasies mean that the relationship between magistrates and youth justice workers in any particular local juvenile justice system will be the subject of continual negotiation. Some magistrates conceive of their major task as balancing the competing claims of deterrence, punishment, atonement and social protection and when they seek advice about sentencing they tend to seek it from the clerk of the court. The clerk is the legally trained professional who is permanently attached to the court and serves as its adviser. Many youth justice workers feel that clerks should confine themselves to the clarification of points of law and not participate actively in decisions about sentences, as happens in some courts (Burney, 1979). The Clerk may not be the power behind the throne, but he or she is certainly the power beside the bench. Magistrates come and go but clerks abide, and in doing so make a deep impression upon the way that 'their' court operates. Whether a youth court is 'tough' or lenient is usually determined by the sentencing advice given to magistrates by the clerk of the court. Clerks are there, notionally at least, to ensure consistency between magistrates, between the youth court and the crown court and to ensure proportionality in sentencing. Although they are often unsuccessful in these endeavours, it is remarkable how each juvenile court takes on a clearly identifiable persona.

The youth justice tariff varies from area to area and this variation is determined by the beliefs and attitudes of the agents of the system, the relationships between them, the availability, or otherwise, of resources and the ages, gender and racial origins of the children and young people who appear in court. Thus, in most local juvenile justice systems, we would expect to find separate sub-tariffs in operation for white boys and black boys aged between 10 and 14, white boys and black boys aged between 14 and 17, boys and girls in both age groups and white girls and black girls.

Justice by race

In the 1980s the number of children and young people entering the juvenile courts and latterly the youth court, as well as the number receiving a custodial sentences once there, declined. This is attributable, in varying degrees, to the success of inter-agency diversionary initiatives, the development of alternatives to custody and a reduction in the numbers of youngsters in the age group. However, as we have noted, this overall reduction obscures the reality that the 1980s and 1990s also witnessed a substantial increase in the confinement of black young people in child-care and penal institutions.

While we have to recognise that part of this increase was attributable to the high proportion of children and young people in the Afro-Caribbean population, research has shown that the discriminatory processing of black and white children and young people in the justice system was a major cause (Taylor, 1982; Berry, 1984; Pitts, 1988). The public controversy generated by this research caused the Home Office, local authority social services departments and the probation service to take stock of the ways they were dealing with black children and young people in trouble. As the 1980s progressed, 'anti-racist' policies, statements and training were instituted in an attempt to rectify the injustices occasioned by racism. Nonetheless, whereas in 1985 Home Office figures indicated that 'West Indian, Guyanese and African' (*sic*) prisoners constituted 8 per cent of the male prison population and 12.2 per cent of the female prison population, by 1992 these proportions had risen to 10.2 per cent and 20.1 per cent ,respectively (Home Office, 1996).

Justice by gender

Relatively few girls enter the youth justice system. (In 1986, 2467 per 100 000 girls aged between 10 and 17 were found guilty or charged for indictable offences compared with 11 571 boys.) The system they enter is different in a number of ways. For one thing it contains fewer options. There is, for example, only one girls' attendance centre in all of England and Wales. Much youth justice provision is geared to the needs of boys and many young women are understandably reluctant to be the only girl at a project. Until 1988, when detention centres were at last abandoned by the Home Office, there were none for girls. This has meant that the tariff for girls has a yawning gap between the discharge and fine at one end, and the much more serious committal to custody at the other. The few girls who do offend persistently may suddenly find themselves 'leapfrogging' from one end of the tariff to the other. This places them at a serious disadvantage in relation to their male counterparts.

　　Another disadvantage they face is that a much higher proportion of persistent female young offenders are deemed to be 'in moral danger' than their male counterparts. While it may be true that, in general, young women are more vulnerable to sexual exploitation by unscrupulous adults, these anxieties about the moral conduct of par-

ticular young women render them much more vulnerable to higher
levels of surveillance or, indeed, custodial confinement irrespective
of the severity of their offences. The double standard towards male
and female sexuality in the social world at large disadvantages young
women when they enter the youth justice system.

Attitudes to young women who offend are also shaped by dominant assumptions about what constitutes appropriate behaviour for
girls and boys. Barbara Hudson (1985) observes:

> Assault, criminal damage, burglary, TDA [taking and driving
> away] and so on are all taken more seriously in girls than boys
> because they are presumed to be so rare and so role-abnormal.
> Shoplifting is the only crime that is considered normal for girls,
> but precisely because it is a woman's crime, shoplifting attracts
> psychiatric explanations in a way that other everyday crimes do
> not.

Girls cannot win, it seems. If they commit typical 'men's' crimes they
are regarded as unnatural, but if they commit typical 'women's'
crimes, they are regarded as irrational.

Influencing the sentencers

Youth justice professionals have sometimes devised ways of making
a greater impact upon sentencing in situations where decisions made
by a bench are either consistently idiosyncratic or discriminatory.
In one area in South London workers monitored the sentences
imposed by magistrates in terms of the racial origins of defendants,
their previous convictions, the seriousness of the offence, and their
home and employment circumstances. An analysis of this material
revealed that black young men were being sentenced more harshly
than other groups. These findings were then presented at one of
their regular meetings with magistrates, their clerks and youth
justice workers, where they were greeted with a mixture of shock,
denial and genuine concern. In this way the workers were able to
mobilise the concern of many of the magistrates in a way which
would have been impossible if they had confined themselves to their
more traditional role of offering opinions and recommendations
about particular cases. As a result of this intervention sentencing
patterns were changed.

There are many examples of magistrates working alongside youth justice workers to ensure a fairer deal for young people. In some areas diversionary programmes and alternatives to custody have been brought into being as a result of the efforts of magistrates and clerks of the court. As with other professional groups who operate in other parts of the youth justice system, it is dangerous to generalise about magistrates and clerks. This said, it has to be acknowledged that youth court magistrates and clerks have often constituted a formidable barrier to progress and reform (Box and Hale, 1986).

If a defendant pleads *guilty* in a youth court, the prosecution will read out the brief facts of the case. There is no need for sworn evidence to be given or for witnesses to be produced. Some defendants may also ask the court for other, additional, offences that they have committed to be taken into consideration. These are offences with which the defendant has not been formally charged. The incentive for the defendant is that all their offences can be cleared up, and they can leave the courtroom in the knowledge that they are no longer at risk of being arrested in connection with them. Generally speaking, offences that are 'taken into consideration' in this way do not lead to a much more severe penalty.

If a defendant pleads *not guilty*, the prosecution will attempt to prove the case against them. The brief facts of the alleged offence will be stated, and witnesses will be called to offer evidence about these facts. The defendant, or their legal representative, has the right to cross-examine witnesses on the accuracy of their evidence. When the prosecution case has been presented, the defendant may give evidence and call their own witnesses who can, in turn, be cross-examined by the prosecution. Alternatively, if a defendant does not wish to be cross-examined, he or she may either remain silent or 'make a statement', which is not on oath. However, since 1994, juries have been allowed to draw an inference from such silence in reaching their decision. In UK courts, the onus is always upon the prosecution to prove the defendant's guilt, 'beyond reasonable doubt', rather than upon the defendant to prove their innocence.

If a defendant has pleaded guilty or been found guilty, a youth court may adjourn the hearing in order that a pre-sentence report (PSR) can be prepared. The purpose of a PSR is to provide additional information about the defendant and their situation in order to assist the court in determining the most suitable method of dealing with them (see Chapter 5). The report will be prepared by a member of the local youth offending team. During this period of adjournment, the young person may be remanded on bail or in care or custody in a remand fostering placement, a local authority secure unit or a prison department remand facility.

If, following a conviction in a youth court, the presiding magistrates feel they have insufficient powers to deal adequately with the offence because of its seriousness, the court may commit the defendant to the crown court for sentencing. A crown court is able to impose a prison sentence of more than six months.

The role of the youth court officer

The youth court seeks advice on the young people passing through it from the youth offending team. To this end youth offending teams will ensure that a youth justice worker is present in the role of youth court officer at every sitting of the youth court. As to the way they should discharge this role, the National Association for Youth Justice (1996) has argued that:

> youth justice agencies have a duty to make services available in all cases involving young people in the criminal justice system, in order to assist the court to come to a decision which is free from discrimination, proportionate to the offence and consistent with the best interests of the young person concerned. In order to contribute to this, there should be a regular and consistent presence in court by a court officer who is familiar with the role, confident in the position and willing to intervene when necessary. Practice should be guided by the need to avoid the use of unnecessary or inhumane incarceration or inappropriate restrictions of liberty.

The major role of the youth court officer (YCO) is assisting courts and young offenders to make sense of each other and ensuring that the young offender's best interests are served in the process. Achieving this requires that the YCO develop skill and expertise in the following areas.

Liaison

The YCO is the representative of the local youth offending team and, as such, he or she is responsible for channelling information between the team and the court. Thus he or she will inform the court verbally of the team's involvement with a particular defendant, inform colleagues of what has happened to the young people with whom they are involved, convey the comments of the magistrates to their colleagues and present their pre-sentence reports (PSRs) in court.

Monitoring pre-sentence reports

Despite the fact that most services have instituted 'gatekeeping' mechanisms for PSRs (see Chapter 5), it will still behove the wary YCO to check all reports to be presented to the youth court to ascertain that:

- they do not contain an inappropriate sentencing proposal, that is one which is either illegal or disproportionate;
- there are no discriminatory or prejudicial statements in the report;
- there is no imprecision or ambiguity in the presentation of information;
- the presentation of the report, plus its spelling and grammar, will not undermine the credibility of the YOT in the eyes of the court.

Before the hearing, the YCO should ensure that all defendants about whom pre-sentence reports have been written are aware of their content. This may entail informing the courts of anything with which the young person disagrees, or of any factual inaccuracies.

Direct assistance to defendants

YCOs will often have to support confused and anxious children, young people and their families, for whom the court appearance will represent one of the most difficult and frightening moments of their lives. The YCO will need to explain what will happen when the proceedings start, who the people in the court are, what the defendant will be expected to do and say, and where they, and their family and friends, should sit. The YCO should also establish whether the youngsters and their families have all the information they need about the charges against them or the sentence imposed upon them and that they understand it. There will be times when a young defendant receives a custodial sentence and it is will often be the YCO who will spend time with the young person in the cells as they deal with the shock.

Influencing the decisions of the court

There are three main ways in which the YCO can influence the decisions of the Youth Court. Firstly, a YCO can provide information about a defendant or facilities in the community, such as the availability of hostel accommodation, with a view to influencing decisions about bail. Decisions about bail are governed by the 1976 Bail Act, which has at its centre the presumption that a court should grant bail unless there are good reasons why this would be inappropriate. These usually concern the likelihood of further offences, interference with witnesses or failure to appear at the next court hearing. Despite the presumption of liberty, some would argue that the spirit of the 1976 Act has been slow to permeate the youth justice system and, in consequence, defendants may be denied bail unjustly. Research suggests that black defendants are especially likely to experience discrimination in this regard (Pitts, 1988). In response to some of these concerns, and the unacceptably high numbers of youngsters remanded to prisons, some youth courts work with *bail information schemes* which provide the court with corroborated factual information about the defendant's circumstances. In this process, the YCO should take care that information to which their agency is party is not passed on to other agencies or used for any purpose other than to facilitate the provision of bail.

Secondly, YCOs can intervene to encourage the youth court to use non-custodial options. Recognising that some young offenders are at particular risk of a custodial sentence, it may be useful to concentrate on them. These young people are likely to be remanded in custody, and the YCO may well interview them to establish grounds upon which to suggest to the youth court that a remand on bail to establish their suitability for a non-custodial penalty might be useful.

Thirdly, the YCO can influence decisions by providing the court with 'stand down reports'. These are verbal reports to the court based on an assessment of the need for a PSR, following a brief interview with the defendant outside the courtroom. 'Stand downs' are undertaken during the proceedings, either at the request of the court or at the suggestion of the YCO, and they encourage the court to remand a case for reports where this would be useful, and eliminate requests for reports in cases where this would be unnecessary, as in the case of low tariff offenders.

Sentencing in the youth court

Sentencing in the youth court, as in the adult courts, represents an attempt to strike a balance between a number of different, and sometimes contradictory, principles. In addition to the considerations it shares with the adult courts, the youth court must also take cognisance of the principle enshrined in sect. 44 of the Children & Young Persons Act 1933, which states that all courts should have regard to the welfare of the child appearing before them, sect. 1(1) of the Children Act 1989, which states that the child's welfare shall be the court's paramount consideration in any proceedings under the Act, and the UN Convention on the Rights of the Child, which requires that, in all actions concerning children in courts of law, the best interest of the child shall be the primary consideration (for these purposes children are defined as being under 18 years of age).

The principles which inform decision-making in the youth court are the following.

Proportionality (the justice principle)

The government's White Paper, *Crime, Justice and Protecting the Public* (Home Office, 1990) asserts that 'punishment in proportion to the seriousness of the crime . . . should be the principal focus of sentencing decisions' (para. 2.2). One of the merits of this principle is its 'fairness', in that everyone convicted of a similar offence can expect a similar punishment. By focusing only upon the offence, however, little account can be taken of the individual offender.

Offenders may be more or less culpable and this has been recognised by the Home Office in its *National Standards*, which require that a YOT worker, in assessing the seriousness of an offence for the purposes of a PSR (see Chapter 5), should pay due regard to aggravating and mitigating factors.

Deterrence

The Crime and Disorder Act (1998) makes no specific mention of deterrence yet it is clear from the available research (Parker *et al.*, 1989; Fagan, 1991) that the desire on the part of magistrates to deter people from committing crime is an important consideration in their sentencing decisions. Deterrence takes two major forms *individual* and *general*.

Individual deterrence, it is argued, is achieved by sentences which are sufficiently punitive to make an offender realise that 'crime does not pay'. The belief in individual deterrence rests upon the assumption that offenders will thereafter be better able to link 'cause and effect' and be deterred from embarking upon further criminal escapades. General deterrence refers to a belief that a punishment imposed upon an individual offender may serve to demonstrate the consequences of criminal behaviour to a wider public who might otherwise be tempted to embark upon a criminal enterprise. Thus, from time-to-time, judges or magistrates may impose 'exemplary sentences' using words to the effect that 'we wish to make it quite clear that this court will not tolerate behaviour of this kind' – a message which is aimed at the rest of us as much as the particular offender being sentenced.

Protecting the public

Sentences designed to protect the public (although they might at the same time have a deterrent effect) are primarily concerned with making it impossible for the offender to reoffend. Typically this would entail custody, although community-based sentences which place restrictions upon the offender's freedom of action, such as curfews and electronic tagging, could also be said to afford the public some degree of protection.

Compensating the victim

In the past the victims of crime have had relatively little acknowledgement from criminal courts. However the Crime and Disorder Act (1998) requires courts to give priority to compensating the victims of crime. There are occasions when this consideration could be in tension with the demands of, for example, deterrence or protection of the public, in that an unwaged prisoner is not in a position to pay compensation and may therefore resort to further crime to do so.

Reparation

This is an allied, but more complicated, concept than the compensation of victims. It involves 'repayment', although not necessarily financial, to an individual victim, for an offence committed against them. However, it also embodies potentially 'therapeutic' elements for the offender, in that they can expunge a sense of guilt and repair the 'broken' relationship with the victim by 'making good' the wrong that they have done. Typically this might occur under the auspices of a reparation order, an action plan order or a community service order, where offenders can be required to confront their victims and/or undertake some socially useful task.

Rehabilitation

A great deal of criminological theory and research evidence suggests that many offences are the direct or indirect result of personal or social disadvantage. Sentences can recognise this by offering the means by which the offender can be helped to function more effectively, thereby minimising the likelihood of further offending.

A balancing act

In reaching their sentencing decisions, sentencers weigh up the seriousness of the offence, public opinion, the attitude of the offender and their social and personal circumstances, the intentions of the law makers and the likely impact upon the offender and the public of any sentence the court might impose. Inevitably the beliefs, values and personal preferences of the sentencer will also play a part in this decision.

Youth offending team members will also have their preferences concerning the principles which should hold sway in sentencing decisions, and these preferences may sometimes be at variance with those of the sentencer. However, whether or not they agree with the perspectives of sentencers, it is important for them to have an awareness of the factors which shape these decisions and the complexity of the sentencing task. The argument that the youth justice worker may put forward in a PSR is more likely to make some impact if it relates to the concerns of the sentencer, and addresses issues to which the sentencer attaches significance.

The range of sentences available to youth courts is sometimes referred to as the 'tariff', since it represents a series of sentencing options (outlined here in approximate ascending order of severity) which are increasingly 'costly' for the defendant. This 'sliding scale' is not necessarily adhered to rigidly by sentencers.

Absolute and conditional discharges

Effectively, an absolute discharge means that a court is taking no action beyond registering a finding of guilt. An absolute discharge would normally only be given when the offence is merely 'technical', extremely trivial, or where there are compelling extenuating circumstances.

In the case of the conditional discharge, the court takes no immediate action on the condition that the defendant does not reoffend during a period specified by the court, up to a maximum of three years. In the event of a reconviction within the specified period, the defendant is liable to be sentenced for the original offence. In 1997, the government announced its decision to remove the conditional discharge from the youth court sentencing tariff, except in exceptional cases. In 1994, 28 per cent of all cases passing through the youth courts were dealt with by an absolute or conditional discharge.

Fines

A fine is a commonly used penalty in the youth court. Each offence has a fixed maximum financial penalty and courts use discretion in fixing an amount up to that maximum. They may be guided in this by such factors as whether the offence was premeditated, the degree of loss or injury suffered by the victim or the degree of vulnerability of the victim. Also relevant is the offender's ability to pay. If immediate payment of a fine cannot be made, courts will frequently enquire into the offender's means, and order payment on a weekly basis. The White Paper, *Crime, Justice and Protecting the Public* (1990) comments that 'it can be difficult to make it clear to the public and to offenders that a particular fine is a fair punishment when another equally culpable offender is given a fine of a different level'. In response to this concern, the Criminal Justice Act (1991) introduced the 'unit fine'. Under this system the number of units an offender is fined is commensurate with the seriousness of the offence, but the value of those units is determined by the offender's weekly disposable income. However this apparently rational strategy was not implemented and has more or less fallen into abeyance. The youth court can order young offenders, or their parents, to pay fines or compensation. The 1991 Act gave the courts duties to order parents or guardians of young offenders under 16 to pay fines, compensation and costs, unless this is considered unreasonable. In fact, few parents are fined because they lack the means to pay. In 1994, fines constituted 10 per cent of youth court disposals.

Compensation orders

A compensation order requires a young person to pay compensation for loss, damage or injury sustained by their victims as a result of their offence (this does not include motor vehicle accidents) A compensation order may be imposed on its own or in conjunction with other orders. The maximum penalty is £2000 per offence and the court must set the amount of compensation with regard to the defendant's ability to pay.

Reparation orders

Reparation is at the core of the present government's 'youth justice reforms' and, under the Crime and Disorder Act (1998), reparation orders are be available for a first or subsequent conviction, for all juveniles, for any offence. The government intends that the reparation order 'will help to show young offenders the harm which they have done to their victims and their communities, and will enable courts to impose punishments which make some amends to the victim'. Indeed the main intention of the reparation order is that it should make some recompense to victims for the harm they have suffered or, if they are in agreement, to the 'community at large'. The court will therefore seek the victim's view of the appropriateness of the recommended form of reparation before passing sentence.

It is intended that reparation will seldom, if ever, be financial, and may include writing a letter of apology or apologising to the victim in person, 'weeding a garden', collecting litter, or doing 'other work to help the community'. However the government has tried to emphasise that it has no desire to reintroduce 'hard labour' by stressing that reparation 'should not involve hard physical work'. Activities will last no longer than 24 hours in total, and should be completed within three months. They will be supervised by a named worker from a youth offending team. The order may be imposed on its own, or it may be combined with a fine, a curfew order, an attendance centre order or a supervision order (without requirements). Courts imposing an action plan order or a supervision order (with requirements) can require that a young offender make reparation as a condition of these orders as a well.

The order will be available to the youth court, the magistrates' court and the crown court. Courts will be required to consider a reparation order in any case in which a compensation order is not imposed. If they decide not to impose a reparation order, they will have to give reasons. If the reparation order is breached, the court may impose a fine or a curfew order, vary the order or revoke the order and re-sentence the youngster for the original offence. If re-sentencing, the court will be required to take account of the extent to which the order has been complied with. It is proposed that the responsible youth justice worker will bring the breach proceedings.

Action plan orders

The 1998 Act introduces a three-month action plan order. Billed as 'a short, intensive programme of community intervention combining punishment, rehabilitation and reparation to change offending behaviour and prevent further crime', this is in effect, a 'super' supervision order. It may require the young offender to comply with educational arrangements, make reparation to the victim and comply with a daily or weekly schedule stipulating their whereabouts and the activities in which they can, or should, engage. It may also require youngsters to stay away from particular places. A fine or compensation order may be imposed alongside an action plan order.

Parenting orders

The parenting order has, the White Paper *No More Excuses* (1997) insists, been designed to 'help and support parents control the behaviour of their children'. It will be available for the parents of convicted young offenders, for the parents of children who are the subject of an *Anti-Social Behaviour Order, Sex Offender Order or Child Safety Order*, and for parents who have been convicted of failing to send their children to school. Parents will be required to attend special guidance sessions, no more than once a week for a three month period. If, however, the court deems it necessary, they may impose additional conditions such as a requirement that the parent take and collect the child from school and that the parent be at home at a certain time every day. These conditions may be imposed for up to a year.

   With the exception of the upper echelons of the probation service, most professional, managers, and not a few magistrates, are extremely sceptical about this measure. For its part, the National Association for Youth Justice believes that, if work associated with parenting and child safety orders is to be carried out at all, it should be done under the auspices of social services department's children and families teams. It also notes that many of the parents who could be made the subjects of a parenting order have already sought assistance from social services departments and voluntary sector projects but have been refused help because these agencies are under-resourced and overworked.

All previous measures to penalise parents for offences committed by their children have been neglected by the bench because they are essentially unjust. As a result, despite the fact that magistrates will be enjoined by the government to impose parenting orders in all cases, unless they state why they are unwilling to do so, it remains unlikely that the parenting order will meet with any more success than other measures which have attempted to inculcate a greater sense of responsibility into the parents of children in trouble with the law.

Supervision orders

It is important to distinguish between supervision orders which arise as a result of care proceedings under sect. 31 of the Children Act (1989), and those which are made in criminal proceedings in the youth court. In criminal proceedings a supervision order may be made in respect of a child or young person between the ages of 10 and 18.

The court can specify the duration of the order up to a maximum of three years. The YOT will be responsible for supervision. It is not necessary for the child or young person to consent to the making of a supervision order. The normal requirements of a supervision order are that the young offender:

- must inform the supervisor of any change of residence or employment;
- shall keep in touch with the supervisor in accordance with such instructions as may from time to time be given by the supervisor and, in particular, that he or she shall, if the supervisor so requires, receive visits from the supervisor at home.

A court may impose additional requirements, namely that the young offender:

- present him/herself to the supervisor or other specified person at a specified place on specified days for up to a maximum of 90 days;
- participate in specified activity on specified days up to a maximum of 90 days;

- remain for specified evenings and nights at a specified place (night restriction) up to a maximum of 90 days;
- refrain from participating in specified activities.

To this list of possible requirements, schedule 12 (23) of the 1989 Children Act adds:

- a residence requirement which may last no longer than six months. For such a requirement to be made, the young person would have to already be subject to a criminal supervision order, and the offence would have to be one which would be punishable by imprisonment in the case of an adult.

From 1998, amendments to the Children and Young Persons Act (1969) will enable courts to impose an element of reparation to the victim and a residency requirement on any young person who breaches, or offends during the course of, a supervision order, if their living arrangements are deemed to have contributed to a significant extent to that breach or offence. Courts will also be able to impose a fine up to £1000. In addition, the provision that the Court must certify that the order is being imposed as an alternative to custody will be removed in order that a custodial sentence can be imposed for the original offence if the supervision order in breached. These changes seem destined to increase the numbers of young people entering secure accommodation and custody.

Attendance centre orders

An attendance centre order is available for offenders up to the age of 21 and it is normally imposed for offences which would be punishable by imprisonment in the case of an adult. The young person must report at the centre at specified times, usually at the weekend, where they will undertake drill, physical education, first aid, crafts, work on literacy or other similar activities. The minimum number of hours that a court can order is 12 and the maximum is 24 for 10–15-year-olds and 36 for 16–20-year-olds. In 1994, 9 per cent of young people appearing before a youth court received an attendance centre order.

Probation orders

Probation orders are similar in many ways to supervision orders and may be made on offenders aged 16 or over. The probation order requires the probationer to be supervised by a probation officer for a specified period of between six months and three years. Probation orders constituted 3 per cent of youth court disposals in 1994.

Community service orders

Community service orders may be imposed upon young offenders of 16 and 17. A community service order has three main purposes:

• *punishment* of the offender by requiring them to perform unpaid work, and the discipline of punctual reporting for work and consequent loss of leisure time;
• *reparation* to the community by requiring the offender to under-take socially useful labour which recompenses the community for the damage and distress caused by the offence;
• it provides work which *benefits the community* which might not otherwise be done.

One of the possible by-products of community service is that it might offer some young offenders a positive, stimulating experience. However the Home Office has indicated that 'the educative and rehabilitative aspects of community service should not take precedence over the need for the offender to comply with the requirements of a court order' (Home Office Circular, October 1988).

The minimum number of hours that can be ordered for community service is 40, the maximum is 240, and these hours should be completed within 12 months of the making of the order. Community service normally takes place at week-ends and offenders usually undertake an average of five hours work per week. The probation service is responsible for the management and administration of the scheme, and probation officers are responsible for reporting non-compliance to the court. Courts may deal with a breach of a community service order by imposing a fine of not more than £400 or revoking the community service order and imposing a different sentence for the original offence. Community service orders constituted 4 per cent of youth court disposals in 1994.

Combination orders

The Criminal Justice Act (1991) introduced a new combination order which has features of both a probation order and a community service order. The Combination order can be imposed upon 16- and 17-year-old offenders. The order requires them to be supervised by a probation officer for a period of not less than 12 months or more than three years and to perform unpaid work for not less than 40 or more than 100 hours.

Curfew orders

The curfew order was introduced in the Criminal Justice Act (1991) and it allowed the courts to require an offender over the age of 16 to remain for a specified period of time in a specified place. The specified period was to be not less than two, or more than 12, hours in any one day, for a maximum period of six months. It was intended that the order should not interfere with the offender's employment or education, or bring them into conflict with their religious beliefs. Provisions in the Crime (Sentences) Act 1997, allows courts to impose curfew orders with electronic tagging on 10–15-year-old offenders. Such a scheme was piloted in Norfolk and Greater Manchester in January 1998. The 1997 White Paper notes that 'The pilots will be carefully evaluated . . . Already, the indications from existing schemes testing tagging on adults are that a curfew order backed by electronic monitoring can help offenders to structure their lives better, and help ensure compliance with other community penalties.'

This is, to say the least, an original interpretation of the experience of existing schemes for adults which have, at times, collapsed into farce, but it also raises serious questions about the relevance and appropriateness of regimes which have allegedly worked with adults in their 20s and 30s to children of 10 or 12. These anxieties are reinforced for many professionals by the fact that curfew orders will not be supervised by YOT workers.

Custodial penalties and custodial remands

The 1997 White Paper *No More Excuses* makes it clear that the government regards the present custodial arrangements for 10–17-year-olds as unsatisfactory:

> the available accommodation is fragmented and regimes vary both in quality and cost; courts' powers to remand young people to secure facilities are inadequate and inappropriate; the sentencing framework can lead to arbitrary outcomes: the kind of institution in which the sentence is served is to a large extent determined by the powers under which the young person is sentenced rather than the needs of the young person; and the structure of sentences does not allow for sufficient emphasis to be placed on preventing offending or responding to progress.

It was for this reason that, in 1997, the new Labour government instituted a review of the whole range of secure accommodation for young offenders and young people held on remand. The purpose of the review was to establish 'how to make better use of existing and planned accommodation to ensure that provision was more consistent and coherent and that regimes tackle criminality and meet the educational and other needs of these young people'. The review covered local authority *secure units*; prison service accommodation, including *young offender institutions* and *secure training centres*; and Department of Health *youth treatment centres*. The White Paper indicates that 'the government wants to see constructive regimes, including education and a high standard of care, to help give young offenders a better chance of staying out of trouble once released'.

Remands to secure accommodation

From 1998 courts had the power to remand to secure accommodation young people aged 12–16 awaiting trial, where it was deemed necessary to protect the public. Prior to this, courts were allowed to remand juveniles to the care of the local authority but were not able to specify that they be kept in secure accommodation. The government recognised that there were insufficient places to meet the likely demand for secure remand places for 12–16-year-olds. To meet this problem, the 1998 Act specifies that 'vulnerable boys', 'those whom a court considers should not be remanded to prison because of their physical or emotional immaturity or their propensity to harm themselves, should be placed in local authority secure accommodation'. However a survey of the remand rescue initiative at Feltham YOI conducted by the London Youth Justice Managers Group in 1998 concludes:

> It is extremely concerning to see such a large number of children who are deemed suitable for a custodial remand, considered 'unsuitable' for secure accommodation. It would appear that increasingly restrictive definitions of vulnerability are being adopted and access to secure accommodation appears to depend upon the willingness or ability of the local authority to locate and fund a placement, rather than a proper assessment of need.

Anticipating the obvious criticism that simply placing those youngsters deemed 'non-vulnerable' in the prison system would render them 'vulnerable', the *No More Excuses* White Paper expressed the hope that 'Regime standards currently being developed by the Prison Service will include provisions to safeguard the welfare of young people, consistent with the need to protect the public and staff.'

Secure training orders

In 1997, the government stated its intention to implement the *secure training order*, introduced by their Conservative predecessors. The *secure training order* may be of between 6 months' and 2 years' duration, is designed for 12–14-year-old 'persistent offenders', and will be served in new secure training centres, as they are completed. To this end, the relevant provisions of Michael Howard's 1994 *Criminal, Justice and Public Order Act* were brought into force in 1998.

Detention and training orders

In 1997, the government announced its intention to introduce a new disposal, available for 10–17-year-olds, called the detention and training order (DTO). A DTO may only be imposed where the offences in question are so serious that 'only custody is justified'. For 10- and 11-year-olds, the government maintains, the power to make an order would be exercised only in response to persistent offending, and only where the court considers that a custodial sentence is necessary to protect the public from further offending. For 12–14-year-olds, the DTO may be imposed only in relation to persistent offending. For 15–17-year-olds, it will be available for any imprisonable offence sufficiently serious to justify custody under the 1991 Act. In the first instance, the government will implement DTOs only for 12–17-year-olds, but there will be a discretionary power for the Home Secretary to introduce the DTO for 10- and 11-year-olds, by an order laid before Parliament, if this proves 'necessary' or desirable' at a later date.

Half of the period of the DTO will be spent in custody and half under community supervision, with provision for shortening or extending the custodial element, depending on the young offender's progress against an agreed 'sentence plan'. Orders will range in length from a minimum of four months to a maximum of two years, with orders of six, eight, 10, 12 and 18 months available. Release dates can be brought forward or delayed depending pon the staff's assessment of the inmate's 'progress':

> In order to respond to good or bad progress, for longer sentences there will be some flexibility in release date. For DTOs lasting between a total of 8–12 months, a young person making good progress against his or her sentence plan might be released from custody a month before the half-way point. For longer sentences, one or two months' early release would be available. Conversely, if poor progress were made, with the agreement of the court, a young offender sentenced to an order lasting 8–12 months could be held in custody for a month beyond the 50% point and one sentenced to 18 or 24 months could be held for one or two months beyond the normal release date. (*No More Excuses*, p.24)

The non-custodial element of the DTO is similarly tough and may be backed up by the home detention curfews announced by the Home Secretary, Jack Straw, in November 1997. A member of the youth offending team, will be appointed at the start of the sentence and he or she will be responsible for post-release supervision of the young person as well. The period of supervision will last until the end of the sentence. A young offender who breaches their supervision requirements during the normal supervision period will be liable to a fine of up to level three (currently £1000) or returned to custody for three months or the remainder of the sentence, whichever is the shorter.

The DTO will be served in any accommodation deemed to be suitable by the Home Secretary. This could mean a Prison Department *young offender institution*, a *secure training centre, youth treatment centre* or *local authority secure unit.*

To claim that the DTO, and the new administrative arrangements which surround it, mark a radical departure from, and a significant improvement upon, what went before strains credulity. Like the action plan order which is, in effect a supervision order executed as the legislators originally intended, the DTO merely offers 'business as usual' except that, unlike previous custodial measures introduced for children and young people, no commitment has been made to the provision of education for those serving longer sentences. Nonetheless, even with a commitment to education and training, the old regimes were insufficient to counter the low morale, lawlessness, despair and occasional suicides which have come to characterise those parts of our penal system to which we consign children and young people who break the law. There is no reason to believe that the hurried measures introduced by New Labour in 1997 will do much to change things.

5

Pre-Sentence Reports

Youth justice workers usually make their first contact with a young offender when the youth court requests a pre-sentence report (PSR) about them. The youth court will request a PSR from the YOT if it is considering a custodial sentence, a reparation order or an action plan order. Magistrates expect youth justice workers, on the basis of their knowledge of the social sciences and methods of intervention, to give 'value-free', expert' opinions and recommendations about the impact of any sentence the court may wish to impose. There is, moreover, often an assumption on the part of the bench that in arriving at their recommendation youth justice workers will have had an eye to the competing claims of 'justice', which must be seen to be done, compensation, or vindication, of the victims, deterrence of other potential offenders, punishment of the wrongdoer, and the needs and best interests of the young offender.

While youth justice workers do usually take these factors into account, the idea that they are disinterested experts is something of a myth. This is because it is based upon the erroneous assumption that a system built upon a foundation of profound ideological and theoretical conflict can generate neutral, or value-free, outcomes. It ignores the tension for youth justice workers between their role as servants of the court and their other role as people who are professionally bound to work in the best interests of the children and young people in trouble who, let us remember, are defined by both the Children Act (1989) and the UN Convention on the Rights of the Child as 'children in need'. When youth court magistrates, acting in what they believe to be the best interest of the community, imprison a young offender, they are almost invariably not advancing the young person's best interest as defined by the Children Act and the UN Convention.

The problem of responsibility

One of the reasons a magistrate will ask a youth justice worker to provide a PSR is to establish the extent to which the young person may be held responsible for their actions. Matza (1964) suggests that this task is problematic in practice because young offenders seldom, if ever, resemble either the free legal subject so dear to the hearts of lawyers, or the determined social object beloved of cognitive behavioural psychologists. He argues that young offenders are neither wholly free not wholly determined. Rather their capacity to exert a free and rational choice is impaired. This helps to explain why many of the young people we meet professionally seem perplexed about how they ended up in so much trouble. It would be naive to ignore the fact that this apparent confusion can be a very convenient rationalisation, but listening to their accounts of what happened we are often left with the feeling that, in some way, the offence happened *to* the young person. There is seldom a sense of a calculating actor embarking upon a freely-chosen course of action.

Most youth crime is, in reality, an ill-conceived shambles. Young people may well be responsible for an offence but it is often hard to extrapolate from their accounts the precise moment at which a choice was made or a decision taken. In their stories, things just happen. Once events are set in train any possibility of exerting control over them seems to evaporate.

Persistent offenders are more often than not people who have little experience of making things happen. They have often been denied the means to become the authors of their own lives. Their social position, having granted them responsibility for nothing, renders them effectively irresponsible. Youth justice workers, by trying to affect their social circumstances, and by confronting young offenders with the issue of choice, attempt to restore to them the responsibility which the limitations of their past experiences may have denied them. Work with young offenders often involves persuading the court to confront a more complex social reality than those suggested by the twin fictions of the *legalistic* and *scientific* world-views, and to accept the validity of their attempts to expand the range of 'solutions' available to young offenders. This latter process can begin in the first encounter between the young person and the worker when the worker is preparing the PSR. In doing this, however, it is important for the worker to acknowledge that the authority he or she carries as an officer of the court will affect the type of relationship he or she will be able to develop with a child or young person in trouble.

Authority

Because most young offenders are able to draw upon a rich legacy of sub-cultural defences in their dealings with people in authority they often have much less of a problem with it than some youth justice workers. The problem for youth justice workers is not, as is sometimes suggested, that their authority creates a barrier to the development of a good relationship with the young offender. That barrier, if it did not exist already, went up as soon as the young person was apprehended. It is the barrier which inevitably separates those who break the law from those who are paid to uphold it. The task of the worker is to respond honestly to these defences which, like all defences, are adaptations to a problematic reality. What both the young person and the worker know is that they would probably never have met if one of them had not broken the law and this acknowledgement is a realistic starting point for the first interview. What is less clear to young people in this predicament, who are often suspicious and frightened, is why they have to talk to a worker and what the worker can do to, or for, them.

Central to this task is the clarification of the choices available to, and the respective responsibilities of, the worker and the young offender. Whatever the vendors of fashionable quick fixes may claim, workers do not stop young people offending. If they do stop, they stop themselves. By engaging the young offender as an active and responsible participant in the production of the PSR, rather than just the passive subject of it, we can help them to develop the capacity to do this. As part of this process it can be useful at the PSR stage to agree a simple interim contract with the child or young person in trouble which covers their own and the worker's rights and responsibilities in the period prior to their court appearance. The contract below was agreed between Beverly, the youth justice worker, and Brian, a 15-year-old on a burglary charge.

Beverly agrees:

1. To help Brian to find a solicitor to represent him in court.
2. That, having gathered the information I need for the production of my PSR, I will discuss my impressions with Brian and give him a chance to correct any mistakes and to discuss in full anything that he doesn't agree with.
3. To then discuss the recommendation I am considering and, if possible, to negotiate it with Brian.
4. To give Brian an honest opinion about the most likely outcome of his forthcoming court appearance and what will be expected of him, including the penalties for non-compliance, if my recommendation is accepted.
5. To give Brian ample opportunity to read my PSR prior to his court appearance, to explain anything he doesn't understand about it and to give him one copy for himself and one for his solicitor.

Brian agrees:

1. To keep appointments with Beverly and any other appointments (at the youth justice centre, for example) which she arranges for me.
2. To decide whether or not to participate in any scheme or programme which I may be offered.
3. To think about what is on offer and to come to a meeting with Beverly with suggestions about the programme which will best meet my needs, or at least that I am prepared to participate in.
4. To discuss Beverly's recommendation and to tell her the measures I am prepared to comply with.
5. To appear in court.

Preparing a pre-sentence report

The *Policy and Practice Guidelines* (1996) of the National Association for Youth Justice indicate that the report writer should always have access to the information about the offence and the defendant held by the crown prosecution service, and should also consult the defence solicitor to obtain the fullest possible picture of the offence. This is particularly important in the case of a not guilty plea.

Reliance solely on the defendant's version of events can lead to an underestimation of the seriousness of the offences with which he or she is charged and this can undermine the credibility of the PSR.

The report should be written in accordance with the current Home Office *National Standard for Pre-Sentence Reports* (1992), and PSR writers should also have access to, and be conversant with, the *National Standards for the Supervision of Offenders in the Community* (Home Office, 1995). When requesting a report, the court will usually indicate its preliminary view of the seriousness of the offences. This information should be conveyed to the report writer, but cannot be binding upon a professional assessment of the facts.

The defendant should be interviewed at length in order to establish all relevant information. It is regarded as good practice to interview the young person in their home on at least one occasion and to interview them both with, and separately from, their parent(s)/guardian(s). A separate appointment should be made to enable the completed report to be discussed with the young person and their carer before the court appearance.

Families

Courts usually want the PSR to give them a picture of a child or young person's home circumstances and family relationships in order to establish whether the family is willing or able to help keep the young person out of trouble. As a result, the PSR writer will usually discuss with the family what they would be willing to do if the court were to require it of them. It is important that, whatever this is, the family has both the capacity and the motivation to do it. The worker who encourages families to agree to unrealistic plans may be setting up both the family and the young person for future failure, a failure, moreover, which could lead to the young person's eventual incarceration. If the family is to engage in some work it must be work on something that they see as a problem. An appreciation of the psychodynamics of school refusal may consistently elude families who may nonetheless fall into a discussion of whose job it is to set the alarm clock with a will. To work effectively with young offenders and their families, or with any other group of people, we need to match our intervention to their concerns and to present it in a way that they can understand and use.

In considering a recommendation the worker can try to engage the young person in a discussion of alternative sources of support and emotional satisfaction. Too often in the past, children and young people in court have been sentenced more severely because their parents are not particularly interested in them. The job of the worker preparing the PSR is not simply to deliver the dismal news about the family but to investigate with the young person alternative sources of support which can be mobilised to compensate for it; to find, in short, another solution.

The school

In preparing their PSR, youth justice workers will usually visit the school attended by the defendant. Magistrates, like most other people, believe that teachers, by dint of the 15 000 hours, or so, that a child will spend in school, will know the child better than other adults (Rutter *et al.*, 1978). Magistrates are therefore prone to accept the school's estimation of the child even when, on a closer reading, the evidence offered may appear to be somewhat dubious. The reality of day-to-day life in an urban comprehensive school often belies the assumed intimacy of the teacher–pupil relationship. Responsibility for pastoral care is delegated to year heads. Responsibility for the control of truancy is assumed by the educational welfare service. Behavioural problems are the domain of the school counsellor, the educational psychologist or the behavioural unit. This division of labour, compounded by staff shortages and the sheer size of the school, can mean that children in trouble may be seen by all but known by none. For the children who hover on the margins of the school it can be a cool and impersonal place. They slip easily through this elaborate network of helping resources which seems to offer everything except the warm and spontaneous relationships which, Rutter *et al.* inform us, make all the difference. It will therefore often fall to the writer of the PSR to point out to the bench that some schools can be highly problematic places for socially deprived and emotionally vulnerable children and young people.

While there is a fairly close correlation between trouble at school and involvement in crime, this relationship cannot be assumed and should be explored afresh in each PSR. A history of trouble in school, particularly if it is punctuated by fixed-term or permanent exclusions, will ring alarm bells in court. Since the publication of *Misspent Youth* (Audit Commission, 1996), the idea that 'school exclusion' is a surefire indicator of future criminality has become ingrained in the professional culture. However, many exclusions are associated with the affront the youngster poses to authority rather than the crime and violence they perpetrate. Interestingly, exclusions for such 'insubordination' appear to be, if anything, more common in high achieving schools in prosperous neighbourhoods where they are employed as a mechanism for 'maintaining standards'. It therefore behoves the youth justice worker to explore the circumstances of such exclusion in some detail.

The educational psychologist

The correlation between difficulties at school and persistent involvement in youth crime suggests that if we are able to identify and deal with the problems a child is experiencing at school this may give us some purchase on the problem of offending. The diagnosis of those problems is the job of the educational psychologist.

Educational psychologists apply tests which provide a comparison of pupils' academic and intellectual capacities and their actual attainment. These tests tell us whether children are 'underfunctioning' and, if they are, what the reasons might be. They make it possible to differentiate between the problems of two equally unhappy children, one of whom is unable to learn because of a cognitive impairment and the other who is unable to learn because of anxieties about his or her family, or the school. On the basis of these tests the educational psychologist is able to suggest the kind of compensatory educational programme, counselling, or indeed school, which in their judgement would constitute the most appropriate response to the problems they have identified.

The psychiatrist

Occasionally youth justice workers encounter young offenders whose behaviour is so bizarre or at odds with reality that the usual ways of understanding their problems and responding to their needs are of no use. In these circumstances youth justice workers may decide to request a psychiatric assessment. There was a period in the recent history of forensic psychiatry when almost all delinquency was seen as a symptom of mental enfeeblement or mental illness. Latterly psychiatry has begun, sometimes somewhat grudgingly, to 'normalise' the offender, recognising that, while a burglar may be a neurotic, psychotic or perfectly sane, so might a politician. But the question of whether, when and in which ways a person's criminality may be a symptom of their mental condition remains. Progressive social-scientific theory has attacked and demolished many of psychiatry's taken-for-granted categories of madness. Yet, although 'psychopaths' have ceased to exist theoretically, we still face a problem when we meet somebody who continues to behave as psychopaths did before they became extinct. In these circumstances a psychiatrist may tell us no more than what we will be unable to do. This is valuable information because it makes our job safer, spares the young person further 'failures' in placements which cannot contain him or her, and pushes us to consider what we believe to be the best of the remaining, often somewhat bleak, options. When youth justice workers seek psychiatric reports in the process of producing their PSR, they usually do so because they are at a loss to know what to do next and hope that a psychiatrist may be able to tell them. Ironically psychiatrists, who may well be able to tell them something of the inner lives of the young people referred to them, are usually unable to throw much light upon the two questions youth justice workers and magistrates most want answered: 'what makes them do it?' and 'what should we do with them?' However sophisticated the assessment, the answers to these questions will be provided ultimately by the magistrate who decides the case, usually on the basis of the PSR recommendation. Psychiatric assessments offer no respite from this responsibility, no access to additional facilities or resources and no easy answers.

PSR writers should, in addition, have access to social services or probation records. In an ideal world, these would contain accurate information and cool assessments. Some do, but unfortunately we cannot distinguish very easily between those which do and those which do not. We must therefore ensure that we do not place undue reliance upon them and that we verify factual information for ourselves.

If the defendant does not speak English an interpreter will be required. Where an interpreter has been used, this should be stated in the report. It is good practice to use an interpreter accredited by the court and the relevant youth justice agencies rather than family members or friends.

The content of the report

The offence

(i)   This section should not be a reiteration of either the young person's or the prosecution's account, but should highlight the nature and seriousness of the offence and the context in which it was committed.
(ii) The analysis should include the circumstances leading up to the offence and factors such as premeditation and the defendant's level of involvement in, and responsibility for, the offence.
(iii) Details of previous offences should not be included unless the circumstances of these offences shed light on aggravating features of the current offence.
(iv) An account of the young person's perception of the offence and their views of its impact on the victim, the harm, damage or cost of the offence should be given. Expressions of remorse or guilt should be noted, and any mitigating circumstances, such as family crises, alcohol, drug or health problems should be brought to the attention of the court. Any aspects of the personal circumstances of the defendant included in the PSR should have direct relevance to the offence(s) about which the PSR is being written.

The young offender

(i)   Where applicable, the fact that the young person has no previous convictions should be stated.

(ii)   The PSR writer should offer an account of the young person's pattern of offending, emphasising any changes in severity or frequency, and linking offences to changes in other areas of the young person's life if this appears to be appropriate.

(iii)   Responses to previous court disposals, with an emphasis on successes and areas of improvement, should be noted.

(iv)   Information about the young person's personal and social life should be included if it throws light upon their offending, their likelihood of reoffending or the likely impact of any proposed community sentence.

(v)   Details of past or present employment, education or community involvement, highlighting any awards, honours and qualifications the young person has achieved or any forms of service to the community they have undertaken, should be included.

(vi)   Where the court is considering the imposition of a fine or a compensation order, information about the financial circumstances of the defendant and their family will be important, particularly if they are experiencing financial hardship.

Risk to the public and risk of reoffending

This section of the PSR presents particular difficulties to the youth justice worker since, at the time of writing, the Home Office *National Standards* take no account of the fact that adolescence is a period of rapid growth and change, that most youngsters pass through a 'delinquent' episode and that, in consequence, present offending may be a poor predictor of future offending. The NAYJ recommends that PSR writers discuss the usefulness of answers to these questions with youth court magistrates.

Conclusion

(i)   The conclusion should flow logically from the rest of the report. If the young person is at risk of custody, attention should be drawn to the likely adverse effects of such a sentence upon them and their family.

(ii)   In proposing a community sentence, it is important to ensure that the option is available and suitable for the young person.

(iii) Where a community sentence is proposed, the PSR should note:

    a) the nature of the proposed order and why it is the most suitable option;

    b) the length of the order and why this particular time period is being proposed;

    c) an outline supervision plan which, insofar as it is practicable, sets out the goals to be achieved by the order and the timescale for their achievement, the frequency of contact between the young person and the worker(s), the proposed content of programmes, venues and the personnel to be involved;

    d) whether, and to what extent, the proposed order will restrict the young person's liberty and influence the likelihood of future offending;

    e) the likely effect of the proposed order on the young person's social and family situation;

    f) the young person's agreement to comply with the order, and his or her understanding of the conditions under which breach proceedings will be initiated.

Anti-discriminatory practice in PSR writing

(i)   Adequate time should be allowed for the preparation of a report. For example, where the report writer is white and the young person is black, time may be needed to overcome the young person's uncertainty or distrust. Similarly the writer may need extra time to develop their understanding of a young person from a different cultural background.

(ii) Overt racist or sexist language is clearly unacceptable, but PSR writers should also be alert to terms or modes of expression which might reinforce racist stereotypes held by a reader of the report.

(iii) Usually, references to race, culture, nationality, colour, country of origin or gender should only be included where they are relevant to the offence, the analysis of offending behaviour or to the proposed sentence. Thus, for example, if the offence may have been racially motivated or committed in response to racist or sexist abuse or provocation, evidence in support of this view should be presented.

(iv)   A young person's experiences of discrimination should be discussed with them to establish whether it contributed to their offending and, if so, evidence of such discrimination might well be included in the report.

(v)   Factors such as gender or racial balance in groupwork programmes and their local availability for black or Asian youngsters or young women should be considered. If they are not available, gaps in resources should be pointed out in the PSR in order to promote equality in sentencing.

Presenting the PSR

(i)   Attendance at court is highly desirable in order that defence solicitors or barristers can be adequately briefed and the report writer is available to answer questions from the court. If the report writer cannot be present, the youth court officer should be fully briefed.

(ii)   The young person should have had time to see the report and an opportunity to discuss it with the writer. The morning of the court appearance is usually far too late to make amendments!

(iii)   The report should be discussed fully with the defendant's legal representative since he or she may only have time to read conclusions or scan the report quickly.

(iv)   If it has not been possible to meet the young person who is the subject of the PSR, no report should be prepared.

6

Working with Young Offenders

The way we were

In our work with young people in trouble our main resource is ourselves. This requires us to think about how these selves operate. To start this process, it may be useful to consider the differences between ourselves as we are today and the way we were at 16 or 17.

- Are our feelings different?
- Do we think differently?
- Are our values different?
- Are our needs different?

When mature students pursuing courses in youth justice have been asked these questions they generally answer that the major differences between then and now are external. Now they have more money, more autonomy and more responsibility, but their thoughts, feelings, values and needs are remarkably similar.

However they also say that they were braver, less compromised, more idealistic, more optimistic, freer and, of course, younger then and that this sometimes makes them envious of the young people with whom they have to deal professionally, or of their own adolescent children. Some say that the struggles with authority, which they first experienced in adolescence, remain unresolved and resurface from time to time as ambivalence and indecisiveness about the position they should adopt with a young person engaged in a similar struggle.

Like a well known brand of Dutch beer, young people can reach parts of us which nobody else can. If we are not careful, work with young people can turn us inside out and split us down the middle.

It can cause us to act like caricatures of ourselves. On the one hand, we may be drawn into collusion with a young person who acts out the battle with authority which we never dared enter at the age of 16; on the other, we may be shocked to find ourselves responding to them in exactly the way our parents did to us, and we vowed we never would.

In this context, maturity consists of recognising the immature or stultified parts of ourselves which are evoked by our encounter with a young person, accepting them and deciding how they will be kept under control. Maturity also involves standing back, separating the self from the problem and not getting annoyed by the inevitable testing out.

Withstanding the wind-up

The affront which some young people in trouble pose to those in authority is just as likely to seal their fate as their offending. We may well, as a result, find ourselves negotiating between the offender and powerful figures she or he has offended. When asked what has happened in these situations our client may, characteristically, reply that she or he was 'only winding the bloke up'. The 'wind-up' is one of the most effective tools available to young people in a relatively powerless position. It allows them to find out a great deal more about us than we would ever willingly reveal and so, in a situation in which we, as adult professionals, have a great deal 'on them', it gives them something 'on us'.

Like the tango, a successful wind-up requires two participants. It is a game which can only be played if both parties join in. Although it may not feel like it, the wind-up will only work if the intended target allows it to, because it is the target who holds the key to its success. The successful wind-up requires the target to take it personally. The moment they do, they are lost and the wind-up will begin in earnest. It is for this reason that workers with young people need to confront, and come to terms with, their own vulnerabilities.

If your ears stick out at right angles from the sides of your head but you do not mind, then adolescent humorists can spend days on end whistling the theme tune from *Dumbo* and it will not affect you; indeed it could become the kind of running joke that speaks of intimacy and affection. If on the other hand you reveal by your reaction that your ears have been the bane of your life, making you a pariah in the playground and a wallflower on the dance floor, you have offered your torturers the tool they need to chip away at your authority, and sufficient material to keep them in paroxysms of mirth for years to come.

It is hard to overstate the importance for the professional worker of not taking hurtful personal remarks personally. They are seldom, in the first instance at least, directed at us because of who we are, but rather because of what we are. Wind-ups are seldom malicious. They are designed as a test to see how far we will go, how much we will take and, importantly, whether or not we have a sense of humour. Children and young people often set considerable store by an adult's sense of humour and this is very astute of them because, as Norman St John Stevas once observed when discussing Margaret Thatcher's personal attributes, 'people with no sense of humour usually have no sense of proportion either'.

The 'testing' of adults by young people is more or less inevitable anyway, but people who have been deprived of the things they most need, as many of the young people we deal with have, can be manipulative and exploitative. If they had not been, they might have got nothing at all instead of the precious little they did get. Like the rest of us they want, and as children they deserve, somebody to love them unconditionally and irrationally, but many of them also know that the people who get closest are in the best position to hurt them. In the resulting emotional melange, harsh words are sometimes spoken and threats are uttered, but that is what we would expect from people who have every reason to be ambivalent about personal relationships. This is why we must confront our own vulnerability and ambivalence. With all of these contradictory emotions flying around it is important that we have a firm grip on our own so that we can remain the steady, predictable, unthreatening adults they need us to be.

What is different about young offenders?

The evidence we have suggests that young people who are persistently or seriously involved in crime are far more likely to have been physically or sexually abused, neglected, rejected or abandoned by their parents, to be poorly educated and excluded from school, to have spent time in care, to be homeless, jobless and living in poverty. This is a problem which has been exacerbated by recent changes in the benefit entitlements for young people living away from the parental home. A disproportionately large number of these young people will be black and their experience of racism may well have compounded the other disadvantages they suffer. They will probably have few close relationships and many of them will abuse, or be dependent upon, drugs, alcohol and other substances.

As a result, in their day-to-day work, youth justice workers, in addition to the problems of crime with which they are required to work, will be faced with some or all of the following, although not necessarily in this order, one at a time, or expressed in words:

- problems of identify and feelings of self worth;
- status frustration, feelings that the skills and abilities they have are underused or undervalued;
- isolation and loneliness;
- questions about sexual and gender identity, masculinity and femininity;
- questions about relationships with parents, partners and, sometimes, the young people's own children;
- the emotional consequences of neglect, rejection, abuse and abandonment;
- low educational attainment and its legacy of feelings of stupidity and inferiority;
- anger, including anger at themselves, which may express itself as self-mutilation or excessive risk-taking, or anger at parents which might take the form of eating disorders;
- sadness and despair, including suicidal feelings;
- violence;
- prostitution and sexual exploitation;
- bullying;
- racism;
- sexism;
- financial problems;
- housing problems and homelessness

This means that, rather than simply administering 'correctional programmes', workers will need to be some or all of the following:

- a non-judgemental supporter who confirms their emerging adult identity;
- a critical ally who holds a mirror up to reality;
- an appreciative professional friend who celebrates their achievements;
- a solid adult who sometimes says no, but always explains why;
- a sounding board who helps them sort out their ideas, priorities and choices;
- an utterly reliable nagger who keeps on at them to do the things they do not want to do even though they are good for them;
- a tireless campaigner against the social and economic conditions which have limited their chances and choices in such a way that violence may sometimes become a problem-solving device.

These are the roles which will be demanded of workers as they embark upon work with children and young people in trouble.

Contracts

Whenever workers are working with young people a contract exists between them. This contract may be implicit, as in the case of the duty social worker who offers a caller advice on welfare rights. No agreement has been signed, but the caller knows he or she has a right to the advice and the worker recognises an obligation to give it. But in more fraught and ambiguous situations, as in work with young offenders, where the roles and relationships are complex and inclined to become confused, explicit contracts may offer both young people and workers greater clarity in their transactions.

As we noted in Chapter 5, a contract is an agreement which specifies the rights and obligations of each of the parties to it. It states what rules exist, what the procedures will be if these rules are broken and the sanctions which can or will be invoked. The contract specifies the roles to be played by the professional workers, the nature and extent of their authority and responsibility, and their accountability and confidentiality. It can state the frequency of meetings between the worker and the young person and what will happen at these meetings.

The great advantage of the contract is that, in the process of drawing it up, each of the parties to it has an opportunity to negotiate its content and exert some control over what is eventually decided. This is particularly important for young people who have always experienced control as something imposed upon them from the outside and boundaries as things they discovered when they crashed into them.

This lack of experience in taking responsibility also means that workers should not encourage young people to enter a contract they will be unable to honour. If, in our anxiety to tie the case up, we steer young people towards situations in which they are unable to meet the demands, we are setting them up for failure. While the contract is notionally an agreement freely and rationally entered into by all of the parties on a basis of equality, and binding on each of them, we should not lose sight of the social reality that in an unequal society some people are in a better position to stick to a bargain than others.

In other words, a contract is a good thing to the extent that it offers greater clarity to all parties and a solid basis from which to work when problems arise. It is a good thing if it allows renegotiation when experience proves that this is necessary. It is a good thing if it requires of the child or young person things that they will be able to achieve and value.

A contract is a bad thing if it is simply a recitation of what will happen to youngsters if they break the rules and offers no possibility for negotiation. It is a bad thing if it is devised only to assuage the fears and anxieties of adults. It is a bad thing if its expectations are out of line with a young person's abilities and allows him or her little opportunity to gain a sense of achievement. It is a bad thing if the young person experiences the contract as just another control or boundary imposed from the outside.

Working with individuals

Just as workers cannot stop young people offending, they cannot solve all of their problems either. Young people usually have to do this for themselves. If we can help them to solve their own problems then we are helping them to exert some control over, and make choices about, their own lives. If we can do this we have helped them to move from a situation they experience as acting upon them to one in which they are taking action in their own right, and to this extent we have helped them to gain a greater degree of independence and autonomy.

This is the primary objective of our work with individual young people, often referred to as counselling. Counselling is not necessarily best conducted in an office or in somebody's home. It is important to create an atmosphere in which young people can say what they want to say in their own way and in their own time. We need to be sensitive opportunists, using the environment imaginatively to create the right circumstances for counselling to take place. It is important to try, as far as possible, to do what *feels* right. There is no instruction book to explain when and how to engage a young person in counselling but we do have intuition, and we should listen to it and trust it.

We can create the right conditions for counselling if we engage in a shared activity. Children and young people sometimes think best and talk best when they are offered opportunities to stop talking, concentrate on something else or change the subject. This may be because they feel less trapped by the problem, or indeed the counsellor. If talking about the problem is not the only option available or seems incidental to the activity. The counsellor for his or her part has to communicate that, while it is fine to talk, it is equally fine not to, and to do this without expressing it as indifference.

Most of the children and young people we work with will have more experience of talking about things than about feelings. As a result conversations that start from the concrete stand a greater chance of success. By and large people can deal with 'what?' questions better than 'why?' questions. 'Why' questions – 'why did you do this?', 'why did she say that?', 'why do you feel like this?' – are often experienced as persecutory. If we stick to 'what' questions – 'what did you do?', 'what did she say?' – we will stay firmly within the experience of the young person and the answers to the 'why?' questions will emerge anyway.

Sometimes children and young people find it easier to talk about the feelings and wishes of a hypothetical third party than about their own: 'What do you think boys like you would feel if this happened?', 'What do you think they'd want to do?' Like shared activity, this technique offers the young person a degree of safety because it does not put them directly under the spotlight. It gives them a 'get-out': they can say what they really feel because they can always claim later that they were not talking about themselves. With younger children, and this can sometimes include 10-year-old young offenders, the third person can be their favourite cuddly toy or cartoon character: 'What do you think Teddy thinks about this?'; 'I bet Spiderman would have something to say about that.'

On the basis of the information gained in the initial session or sessions we can help the young person to define their need or difficulty more clearly, identify the choices which are open to them, and plan what they are going to do about it and how we are going to help them do it. Our capacity to analyse and clarify may be the most important resource we can offer young people. This conceptual reorganisation of the problem can help to transform the insoluble chaos the young person is experiencing into a series of small achievable tasks and this may in consequence transform despair into optimism. We offer our analysis and clarification by summarising, paraphrasing and reflecting.

When we summarise we check with the young person that we really have heard what they are trying to say. Our summary will inevitably be *our* understanding of what has been said. When we offer the young person a summary we are not offering them what they said but what we *heard*. If we have listened carefully and sensitively, however, we may find that we are giving them back what they really *meant* rather than what they actually said. Paraphrasing allows us to identify the key themes in what is being said and offers the young person and the worker a shared shorthand to use in talking about complicated situations. When we reflect back we hold up a mirror for the young person to stand back and look at themselves. We offer them our understanding of what they have said to us in order that they can explore it further: 'Do you mean you felt guilty?', 'It sounds like you don't actually like your boyfriend very much.' In doing this we use intuition to feel what it is like for the young person and this is a perfectly proper way to work. It only becomes improper if we fail to check the information supplied to us by our intuition with the young person.

Individual counselling is a spiral. The young person speaks, we summarise, paraphrase and reflect. Together we define the problem and identify the components of a solution. We establish priorities and specify the tasks to be undertaken, who will do them and how they will be done. Together we evaluate how the tasks have been done and we offer the young person feedback about their achievements in order to give them the strength and confidence to keep on with the next set of tasks. Faced with these tasks and an ever-changing situation, the young person speaks . . . we summarise, paraphrase, and reflect . . . until, we hope, one day they do not need us anymore because, through our work, we have encouraged them to develop their own ways of making sense of their lives and sufficient confidence and self-esteem to trust and rely upon themselves.

Working with friends

For many young people the transition from dependence to independence is supported by a small group of friends or one best friend. These relationships sometimes come to assume a greater significance than family relations and can last a lifetime. Interestingly, when young people are invited to attend an interview with a youth justice worker, they often arrive with a friend. This can pose a problem, but it also presents an opportunity. It may be that we will be able to engage the young offender more effectively if their friend becomes part of the interview. It can, for example, help to forestall the type of gruelling non-interview in which an increasingly desperate worker tries to convey his or her message to a petrified, and hence effectively deafened, young person.

Friends can help out with the answers. Not being officially in trouble themselves, but often 'knowing the form' nonetheless, they tend to feel more relaxed and better able to ask the important questions which their friend, who is 'on the spot' would not dare. They can also act as interpreters, often delivering our message far more succinctly than we are able. Our friends usually see us more realistically than we are able to see ourselves, and recognise patterns in our behaviour of which we are barely aware. They can confront us with what we are doing more directly than any professional would dare, yet despite this, or possibly because of it, young people who apparently pay little or no attention to anybody else will often listen to their friend.

Girls are more likely to associate with one or two best friends than a larger peer group. Too often we have tried to shoehorn girls into fabricated peer groups of our own construction in the mistaken belief that we are reproducing the 'natural' milieu in which girls could be encouraged to get on with the developmental task. Men engaged in work with young offenders have often failed to ask, or listen to, the women with whom they work and the young women for whom they work. As a result they have missed some important information which has serious implications for our interventions. Girls are often much more able than boys to talk about their feelings and they tend to do this with their best friend. Sexism has often prevented us from seeing the 'best friend' relationship as a target for intervention with young women in trouble. Marilyn Lawrence (1983) writes:

> when I first began working with young women, rather than adults, in a counselling context, I was amazed at the ease with which 13 and 14-year-olds were able to talk to me. I had not expected their mature and thought-out understandings of their own social worlds, or the fact that they would be willing to share it. (p. 27)

She continues:

> I suspect that co-counselling has a great deal to offer. It is, after all, exactly what best friends, at their best, engage in anyway. It is also a powerful way of indicating that listening carefully to what other women say, and in return, being listened to, is a proper and important activity. If twenty years of women's liberation hasn't taught us that it hasn't taught us anything. (pp. 28–9)

It is not that boys are never amenable to one-to-one or 'best friend' interventions. Many boys are not members of an identifiable peer group and are sometimes eager to discuss issues with a disinterested adult. It is rather that girls, by dint of socialisation, opportunity and a tendency to 'mature' earlier than boys, tend to be more responsive to interventions aimed at their thoughts and feelings about themselves.

Working with families

For effective family work to be possible certain conditions must obtain. It is necessary that family members, particularly parents, should be concerned about the 'problem'. There should be a fair level of agreement between the family and ourselves about the nature of the problem, and this 'problem' should fall within the terms of reference of our agency. The young person should still be an effective part of the family group and there should be some indication that family members have both a willingness and some ability to deal with things differently. We should be aware of whether the family has been offered family work before, whether or not they accepted it and, if they did, what the outcome was. We also need to consider whether or not we have the necessary skills to tackle all the potential levels of difficulty of the work.

Occasionally when we visit the home of a child or young person in trouble all of these conditions will obtain. We will meet a mother and a father who are eager to collaborate with our attempts to discover the cause and the remedy of their child's behaviour and who have both the desire and the capacity to confront the problems which may have led to their child's offending. More often, we will meet parents who are perplexed about their child's behaviour, ambivalent about our intervention and uncertain about what, if anything, might be done about it.

Sometimes, as we have noted, we will meet parents who express no concern about the offence or our intervention or their child. This may be a consequence of depression, deprivation or despair, particularly if the parents were themselves deprived as children. We all need to experience inclusion, affection and a sense of control over events. If the parents have been deprived in these areas and see their child having these needs met by us, they may well become jealous. This might, of course, offer us a point of entry to the parents if we are prepared to respond to their needs as well, but it may also mean that the parents attempt to sabotage the child's participation in any supportive network we have helped to construct. In these circumstances we may choose to use our authority to deflect the resentment away from the child and onto ourselves. We can tell the parents that the child is required, as a condition of his or her court order, to comply with any directions we give them. In this way we may minimise the guilt and anxiety the child feels if they are enjoying themselves because we have told them that they have to do it. This *may* serve to protect them from being punished for their enjoyment, but it may not and we need to watch these situations carefully. This practice is by no means ideal but, although we are working despite the family, we are, paradoxically, still working with the family. Virginia Satir (1964) writes:

concern with the family as a unit does not necessarily involve working with the whole family as a group, all the time. It is a focus for work, not necessarily a method of working. It simply means that, whatever is being done to help any member, the needs of the whole group, and the difficulties that any particular member has in meeting or reconciling himself or herself with these needs should be the primary focus.

We do not go through these elaborate contortions to keep the child in the community out of an irrational distaste for residential institutions but because research tells us that levels of offending often rise in the wake of a spell in care or custody, and that the removal of a child or young person from a problem home for more than a few weeks makes it very difficult to place them back in it. This matters because even the best residential establishments for young offenders are seldom able to meet their emotional needs as well as what we might regard as fairly negligent families. We struggle to keep the child at home when we do, not because of an uncritical emotional or ethical devotion to the nuclear family either, but because it is usually not as bad as the alternative. Whatever problems a youngster may experience within the family can be seriously compounded if they fall foul of the law.

Young offenders who have 'unco-operative' parents tend to be punished for it. As in schooling, the child or young person whose parents appear interested in, and concerned about, their child's progress tend to be regarded by adult professionals as, at least potentially, interested and concerned themselves. Conversely, the children of parents who are reluctant to speak to professionals and loth to appear at court tend to he viewed as having a *poor* prognosis. Parental co-operation and interest, or their absence, are regarded as a significant factor when magistrates are deciding whether a child or young person should be placed at home or in an institution. In court the attitude of the parents may make the difference between a custodial and a non-custodial sentence.

If, in these circumstances, we wish to defend the young person, and natural justice as well, we will have to ensure in our PSR that any evaluation of the parents is not automatically and unthinkingly translated into assumptions about the child or young person. We will also need to develop, through a process of inter-agency co-operation, a viable network of support which responds to the needs of, and offers a better self-image to, the child.

Inter-agency co-operation

With the establishment of youth offending teams, inter-agency co-operation in the youth justice system in England and Wales has become a legal requirement. This should lead to greater efficiency and effectiveness. However, inter-agency work is not without its difficulties (Crawford, 1998). As we have already noted, a feature of work with socially marginalised or emotionally deprived young people is the degree of conflict it can sometimes generate within professional workers. It can also do this within a team, an agency or between agencies. This is not the place to explore the extent to which conflictual professional relationships mirror the conflictual relationships in which they are required to intervene. What is clear, however, is that such conflict usually militates against the best interests of the young people involved.

In high stress situations, differences of priority, orientation and opinion between workers about the most appropriate course of action can come to assume a far greater significance than they would, on the face of it, appear to merit. What might, in other circumstances, be seen as helpful advice can, in this situation, be received as unwarranted criticism and interference. The ever-present tendency for those with case responsibility to minimise the risks to themselves can result in them resenting the 'interference' of 'outsiders' who have nothing to lose. Even where responsibility is shared, anxiety can heighten disagreements about the value and likely outcomes of the strategies proposed. One of the consequences of this can be that, in a situation which may require unity, some workers will be more committed to a joint strategy than others.

These problems are compounded when there is no mechanism for resolving disputes or negotiating a compromise between professional peers. If discussions reach an acrimonious stalemate, the idea of a shared strategy may soon be abandoned or the problem pushed up the hierarchy for an, inevitably unsatisfactory, management decision. If this latter option is pursued, it then becomes possible to blame 'management' for yet another 'bloody stupid decision' and this can then reunite the professionals in their opposition to it.

What all this adds up to is a plea for openness and honesty between agencies and team members and a commitment to shelving the 'macho-correctionalism' which characterises the professional style of some workers with young people in trouble. Some young people will test the boundaries of the professional relationship very vigorously by presenting threatening or self-damaging behaviour to workers. This often makes workers frightened, yet as professionals they feel that they should be able to cope. As a result, unless they are able to be honest about their apprehensions, they may develop a variety of, not always very useful, strategies to deal with the onslaught of the young person and the fear and anxiety it induces. Good practice involves having space to work creatively and take calculated risks with young people who might be difficult to engage, in the knowledge that managerial and peer support and professional supervision are available.

Effective teams stick closely to the principle that confidentiality belongs to the agency and they tend to share information about positive developments in young people's lives as well as questions of dangerousness, violence or abuse. Information should be communicated systematically, rather than inadvertently, to all team members, including administrative staff. Effective teams negotiate their roles and the boundaries they intend to maintain in their work with individual young people. Many of the young people with whom youth offending teams have contact have never been given accurate feedback about themselves and the impact of their behaviour. They have not experienced the imposition of realistic and consistent boundaries, so a coherent response from all team members is crucial.

Conclusion

Even in traditionally high-crime inner-city neighbourhoods it is usually a small minority of children and young people in the 10–17 age group who give cause for serious concern because of their involvement in crime or violence. Most children and young people grow out of crime. Adolescents change, sometimes very fast. A new job, a new teacher, a new girlfriend or boyfriend, or just growing up and recognising the consequences of their actions can make the difference. If we can hang on, and encourage others to hang on as well, we can often see a child or young person through their offending and out the other side (Rutherford, 1986). It is within this situation of change and flux that we develop our face-to-face work with children and young people in trouble. Our responses to young offenders must reflect the reality of growth and change. The very different activities of playing *Monopoly* with a girl of 12 and working with her as a young woman of 14 on the question of whether she should or should not embark upon a sexual relationship are separated by a matter of months. We have to develop relationships in which youngsters feel free to be both children and adults without anxiety or shame. One of the most important things that adult professionals can offer children and young people is a place where they can practise growing up while not having to be grown up.

7

Preventive Work in the Community

The renaissance of prevention

The renewed enthusiasm for 'prevention' in youth justice in England and Wales in the mid-1990s grew out of a disillusionment with the apparent inability of the 'systems management' strategies of the 1980s to contain or reduce youth crime (Audit Commission, 1996). In the 1980s many local authority youth justice sections abandoned both preventive work with young people 'at risk' and 'in need' and more intensive long-term work, including day-care provision for young people who would otherwise be in residential care or custody. In its place they developed a far more narrowly focused strategy of 'systems management' which concentrated upon time-limited, offence-oriented work with 'high tariff' adjudicated offenders. This change was due in part to the currently popular view that in intervening too early, or too intensively, in the lives of youngsters in trouble, one might stigmatise them in ways which would draw them deeper into the justice system (Cohen, 1979; Thorpe *et al.*, 1980). This political/theoretical rationale notwithstanding, the major factor in this narrowing of the scope of youth justice in the 1980s and 1990s was cutbacks in local government expenditure which led to a progressive reduction in the human and material resources available to youth justice workers. These cuts were paralleled, and compounded, by serious staff reductions in the educational social work service, school counselling, pastoral care, home–school liaison and home tuition and the closure of off-site units, many child and family guidance clinics, the bulk of youth service establishments, and those voluntary sector projects not involved in statutory youth justice or child protection work.

It was against this backdrop of a steady deterioration in the services for children and young people in need and in trouble that the Inner London Youth Justice Principal Officers Group convened to produce their *Statement of Principles and Practice Standards* (ILYJS, 1995), which, in turn, spawned the *National Protocol on Youth Justice* promulgated by the Association of Directors of Social Services in 1996. Alongside these developments, the late 1980s and early 1990s witnessed a widespread concern about the growth of youth crime in general and violent youth crime in particular. This meant that youth crime and its prevention became a central political issue in the run-up to the 1997 general election.

The recent history of crime prevention in the UK

The contraction of youth justice and allied services and the dominance of 'systems management' approaches in the 1980s were paralleled by the emergence of a new crime prevention strategy in the Home Office (Clarke, 1980). At the core of 'situational' crime prevention was the belief that crime could be effectively reduced by eliminating or reducing opportunities for its commission, rather than intervening to change the behaviour, beliefs, values or social circumstances of perpetrators.

Characteristically, situational crime prevention brought together local authority housing, planning and amenities departments, the police, local businesses and transport authorities with citizen groups, to devise strategies for reducing the vulnerability of the physical environment through 'target hardening', the application of better locks, better lighting, the introduction of concierge systems, janitorial patrols, 'sleeping policemen' and so on. However, by the late 1980s and early 1990s, the efficacy of situational crime prevention was being called into question. While, on the one hand, situational crime prevention had revealed a tendency to displace crime into other areas or onto other groups who had not been the beneficiaries of 'target hardening' initiatives, on the other, it had made little apparent impact upon the rapidly rising crime rate.

What situational crime prevention had done, however, was to establish the idea that, to be effective, crime prevention must become the responsibility of a broad range of agencies and not just the police. This was first signalled by Home Office Circular (8/84) which endorsed the idea of 'inter-agency co-operation' in crime prevention. In 1990 the government issued a further interdepartmental circular and, in 1991, the Home Office Standing Conference on Crime Prevention published *Safer Communities: the Local Delivery of Crime Prevention Through the Partnership Approach* (the Morgan Report) (Home Office, 1991). The Morgan report was not particularly enamoured of situational crime prevention but it was persuaded that the key to effective crime prevention lay in partnership. The report recommended that:

- local authorities, working in conjunction with the police, should have responsibility for the development and stimulation of community safety;
- the development of a community safety strategy should take place at the highest tier of local government;
- local multi-agency partnerships should give particular attention to the issue of young people and crime in preparing a portfolio of crime prevention activities;
- wherever possible a co-ordinator with administrative support should be appointed in each unitary or county-level local authority;
- central government should provide a community safety impact statement for all new legislation and major policy initiatives.

The report also gave currency to the term 'community safety':

> The term 'crime prevention' is often narrowly interpreted and this reinforces the view that it is solely the responsibility of the police. On the other hand, the term 'community safety' is open to wider interpretation and could encourage greater participation from all sections of the community in the fight against crime. (para. 3.6)

Unsurprisingly a government bent upon reducing expenditure upon, and restricting the powers of, local authorities rejected Morgan's key recommendations out of hand. Thus, instead of the coherent national structure proposed by Morgan, community safety in the early 1990s comprised a patchwork of unrelated initiatives which depended largely on voluntarism, local political will and a perpetual hunt for resources for their realisation. As Bright (1991) observed, the government was 'attempting to tackle a multi-billion pound problem with an under-resourced package of voluntary action, multi-agency co-operation and short-term, centrally con-trolled projects' (p. 81). As a result, much of what passed for com-munity safety in the early 1990s was merely public relations whose impact, if any, was upon the fear of crime rather than crime it-self (Bright, 1991). While 'community safety' continued to infuse political rhetoric, the major thrust in crime control from 1992 concerned the development of an increasingly punitive criminal justice apparatus.

In its report, *Misspent Youth: Young People and Crime*, the Audit Commission (1996) argued for forms of crime prevention which focused upon the behaviour, attitudes and social circumstances of young people in trouble. This was a response to its findings that very little preventive work was done with youngsters when they first became involved in crime and that most of the billion pounds spent on youth justice was, in fact, devoted to processing young people through the courts.

The Audit Commission's principle recommendation was that resources should be shifted from the processing of young offend-ers towards effective prevention and timely intervention. Like the Morgan report, *Misspent Youth* recommended that the government should require local authorities to convene inter-agency groups and that these agencies should be given a duty to co-operate.

New Labour, new responsibilities

In the campaign that preceded the 1997 general election, the Labour Party indicated that, if it were to form the next government, it would bring forward proposals on community safety which accorded with the recommendations in the Morgan report. True to this manifesto pledge, in September 1997, the government circulated a consul-tation document which indicated that the future administrative arrangements for community safety would form part of the Crime and Disorder Act (1998). The consultative document (Home Office, 1997) proposed that:

- local authorities and the police service would be given new duties to develop statutory partnerships to prevent, and help reduce, crime;
- the implications of all decisions by local authorities, for the

reduction of crime and disorder, should be considered by elected members and council officials in the same way that the financial or equal opportunities implications of decisions are currently considered;

- this new duty should rest jointly on the district/unitary authority (or London Borough), the chief officer of police and, where the two tier structure still exists, the county council, and that the key partners are to have an equal stake;

- this duty would require these bodies to form a leadership group and jointly conduct an audit of crime and disorder in their area, consult collectively with local agencies on targets and timescales for reducing crime and publish a local community safety strategy;

- the Home Secretary would be given a reserve power to call for a report from the leadership group on its discharge of any of these duties;

- the government would also specify agencies which must be involved in the audit, planning and delivery process;

- there would be a legal obligation on the leadership group to produce targets, publish them and report the outcome.

The 1998 Act places responsibility for community safety with local authorities who must produce 'targets' for a 'corporate strategy'. However the consultative document also asserts that the proposals do not amount to the creation of a new service, but are a matter of 'putting crime and disorder considerations at the heart of decision making' (Home Office, 1997, p. 11). As to the costs of this endeavour, the paper suggests that there will be no additional money from central Government for these new duties, but that substantial savings should result from these new arrangements. If, as the Audit Commission suggests, a combination of greater efficiency and effective youth crime prevention generates significant savings in the one billion pound youth justice budget, these savings might usefully be redirected towards community safety. At present, however, there are no plans to effect such a transfer. As Adam Crawford (1998) notes:

> The question of the relationship between designated crime prevention funding and wider mainstream social and criminal justice funding is a particularly vexed one ... there is little point in setting up pilot or demonstration projects if they collapse at the end of the funding period due to lack of mainstream support.

The economic stringencies of the late 1990s will probably mean that individualistic, rather than socioeconomic, explanations of youth crime will continue to dominate political debate and this will lead to the development of forms of preventive intervention which focus primarily upon individual offending. It is therefore important to look again at the idea of prevention in order to gain a better understanding of its potential and its limitations.

The nature of prevention

The literature on prevention distinguishes between:

- *primary prevention*, which attempts to modify or eradicate *criminogenic* aspects of the social, economic and physical environment;
- *secondary prevention*, which attempts to reduce the risk of future involvement in crime by individuals or groups thought to be 'at risk' because of social, economic, personal or family characteristics or their physical or social environment; and
- *tertiary prevention*, which focuses upon the behaviour, beliefs, attitudes, values, modes of thinking and opportunities available to individuals or groups who are already involved in crime.

While these distinctions are useful in enabling us to think through the levels at which a youth crime prevention strategy might operate, Graham and Bennett (1995) argue that, in practice, practitioners and policy makers tend to think in terms of:

- *criminality prevention*, which focuses upon actual offenders and attempts to change their motivation and behaviour;
- *situational crime prevention*, which focuses on modifications to the physical environment to reduce opportunities for crime; and
- *community crime prevention*, which involves a broad range of individuals and agencies in a variety of initiatives, spanning primary, secondary and tertiary modes of prevention.

The rest of this chapter will focus mainly upon primary and secondary prevention, while the next chapter will deal with tertiary, or 'criminality' prevention. Situational crime prevention, because it does not involve specific interventions with young offenders, will not be dealt with in this book, but a full discussion of its potential and its limitations can be found in Marlow and Pitts (1998).

Crime does not occur in a vacuum. As Table 7.1 indicates, crime rates vary from country to country and this variation is determined by broader, political and economic factors (Messner and Rosenfeld, 1994; Pitts, 1998).

We know that the most violent and crime-ridden western societies are those characterised by the greatest disparities in wealth and opportunity (Segal, 1990; Esping-Andersen, 1990; Currie, 1991; Messner and Rosenfeld, 1994). We also know that the negative social effects of unbridled market forces can be ameliorated by social and economic policy (Currie, 1991).

Primary prevention

It follows, therefore, that a country which wished to commit itself to the reduction of crime would develop a strategy of primary prevention which utilised major policy areas to 'strike at the roots' of crime. In what follows, the key features of such policies in the areas of income policy, employment policy, urban policy, family policy and youth policy are outlined.

Income policy

A nation wishing to use income policy to put a brake on crime would:

● institute a realistic statutory minimum wage, set in accordance with the average levels of consumption within that society;

Table 7.1   Rises in recorded crime rates,
1987–95

Austria	27.3%	Germany (W)	15.4%
Belgium	33.0%	Greece	0.0%
England and Wales	31.0%	Italy	15.5%
Finland	19.6%	Netherlands	8.0%
France	22.0%	Sweden	2.8%

Source: Criminal statistics (abridged) HMSO (1995).

- institute a system of progressive taxation in which income discrepancies were gradually eroded by financial and social resource transfers between citizens;
- institute systems of social benefits which allowed all citizens, irrespective of employment status, to participate fully in the social, cultural and political life of the nation.

As Table 7.1 above indicates, in Sweden, where policies of this nature has been pursued for many years, the rise in the recorded crime rate is amongst the lowest in Europe.

Employment policy

Richard McGahey (1986) suggests that the key characteristic of neighbourhoods with high levels of crime and violence is an absence of adults in reasonably paid, superannuated, 'primary sector' employment. Steady jobs for adults promote demographic stability which enhances a neighbourhood's capacity to exert informal social control and offer social support. They also create pathways through which adults can introduce the next generation into the labour market, thus giving them a 'stake in conformity'.

In what had been a high crime housing estate in a Parisian suburb, with a great deal of drug-related violence, a policy was devised which prioritised local jobs in the public and voluntary sectors for local people in order to reduce local unemployment and promote interaction between neighbours. Meanwhile, the *Mission Locale* (the local office of the French equivalent of the Department of Trade and Industry) worked to attract industry to the area and commissioned a national voluntary youth welfare and training agency to develop long-term youth and adult training, an extensive programme of social and cultural activities and establish a residential foyer for children and young people from the neighbourhood who were unable to live with their families. These types of policies were pursued in most of the socially deprived, high crime neighbourhoods in France in the 1980s . . . did they work?

In 1981 in both Britain and France 3 500 000 offences were recorded by the police. However, by the end of the 1980s, the number of offences recorded in Britain was approaching 6 000 000 while in France, between 1983 and 1986, there was a decline in recorded offences to around 3 000 000, where it remained for the rest of the decade (Parti Socialiste Français, 1986; De Liege, 1991; Gallo, 1995). In Britain, where there was no concerted attempt to change the social conditions associated with crime in general and violent youth crime in particular, crime rose fastest in the poorest neighbourhoods (Hope, 1994). However, in France, it was in precisely these neighbourhoods that the fall in the crime rate was most marked (King, 1989; De Liege, 1991; Pitts, 1988). Sweden also operates an active labour market policy in which public resources are used to generate reasonably paid, dignified skilled work for young people and adults.

At the time of writing, the British government is introducing a New Deal programme, based on the US *Workfare* initiative. One of its aims is to reduce crime. New Deal will fund 250 000 places in short and medium-term subsidised employment in the private, public and voluntary sectors, revamped government training schemes and college and university courses. Young people who fail to take up one of these options will face substantial cuts in their benefits. Whether New Deal can produce enough of the right type of permanent primary sector jobs in the right areas and, if it does, whether the often poorly motivated and poorly educated youngsters who constitute the bulk of apprehended young offenders will fit into them remains to be seen. Whereas in the UK the New Deal jobs will be subsidised for six months, a parallel scheme in France guarantees a subsidy for five years.

Urban policy

It is clear that in the UK in the 1980s the shortage of decent public housing and the effective 'dumping' of socially and economically deprived families on the worst housing estates contributed significantly to the growth of crime in general, and interracial youth violence in particular. If, therefore, one wished to reduce violence, housing suggests itself as a prime target for intervention. On the French housing estates referred to above, housing policy aimed to locate the children and relatives of local residents in local accommodation in order to strengthen ties of friendship and kinship, stabilise the neighbourhood and strengthen indigenous sources of social control. On the estate where the present author undertook

this research, this was decided by the locally elected Neighbourhood Council which was established, through negotiations with the
mayor's office, as an additional tier of local government in the
quartier. All residents of 16 and over, irrespective of immigration
status, were allowed to vote for the Neighbourhood Council and
around 40 per cent did. Some 75 per cent of the population of the
Flaubert Estate were of North African, Central African, Turkish or
Portuguese origin and most had never voted before in any French
election. As a result of this policy, however, many apartments were
overcrowded, being unsuitable for the many large families on the
estate. However new, larger, council homes and a new hospital are
now being constructed alongside the estate. One of the consequences of these developments had been that requests for transfers
off the estate had dwindled, while the waiting list for transfers onto
the estate had grown significantly.

On the East London housing estate, with which the Parisian estate
was being compared as part of a comparative study of responses
to youth crime (Pitts, 1998), the Housing Department operated a
system of housing priority points, determined on the basis of social
need. This was a policy which was increasingly difficult to implement
in the face of the erosion of good quality local housing stock occasioned by central government's 'right to buy' strategy and 'tenant
incentive schemes'. This meant that 'disruptive' tenants, those who
did not pay their rent regularly, the homeless, often young single-
parent and Bengali families, and successive waves of refugees were
allocated to the unpopular and underused tower blocks on the estate
which were notorious for their high crime rate and drug dealing.
This had produced a less stable neighbourhood with fewer ties of
kinship and friendship. One of the consequences of this was that the
neighbourhood had one of the highest levels of racial attacks in the
borough and support for the neo-fascist British National Party
amongst established white families was strong.

Family policy

Whereas the family, in many European countries, is a 'public issue',
in the UK it is emphatically a 'private trouble' (Mills, 1959; Chester,
1994). In most northern European states the family, its economic,
educational, cultural and social needs, and its capacity to bring up

its children are deemed to be a legitimate concern of governments. Thus support for the family in its child-rearing role, via substantial cash transfers and the provision of universal support services free at the point of access, are not uncommon (Esping-Andersen, 1990; Ginsberg, 1992; Cooper *et al.*, 1995). In the UK policy responses to the family are characterised by a deep ambivalence. It is for this reason that Britain has no explicit family policy which might serve as a vehicle for the prevention of youth crime. As Chester (1994) observes:

> There is a contradiction between the belief that the State should not encroach upon the autonomy of the family and its perceived duty to ensure that family care of dependants and socialisation of the young is adequately conducted. By acting indirectly, abstaining from proclamation of general objectives for the family, and intervening only against families which can be defined as malfunctioning or in need, the State has been able to minimise controversy regarding its intrusions. (p. 227)

The Crime and Disorder Act (1998) marks a deeper involvement by the state in family life with the introduction of the child safety order and the parenting order. However these measures, which redefine in quite radical ways what the proper concerns of the state and the law should be, are to be invoked only as a means of instilling discipline into socially deviant families. One might add that the government's bungled attempt to get single parents back to work by cutting their benefits in 1998 did not bear the hallmark of a positive vision of the family either.

Youth policy

Throughout the post-war period, politicians, academics and professionals have argued for a coherent, integrated national youth policy. Instead young people, their needs and their problems, have been dealt with by a multiplicity of agencies and organisations, most of which do not specialise in work with the young. Since the early 1980s, however, there has been growing concern in government about the relationship between permanent, structural youth unemployment and mounting youth homelessness, youth prostitution, youth suicide, social polarisation in secondary education, the 'ghettoisation' of socially disadvantaged families, urban decline and youth crime and civil disorder. This has prompted a previously unheard of degree of co-operation between senior civil servants in the key ministries. One of the results of this has been the emergence of a new wave of 'corporate' policy initiatives, of which the government's Social Exclusion Unit is a good example. This culture of 'corporatism' also infused local authorities in the late 1990s and its fruits can be found in the youth offending teams brought into being by the Crime and Disorder Act (1998) and the local authority–police–voluntary sector corporate community safety strategies which the Act requires them to develop. This, somewhat belated, attempt to deal with the problems confronting young people in a 'holistic', we could say intelligent, way is to be welcomed although, at present, there are few attempts to trace these problems back to their roots in the radical political, social and economic changes which have occurred in most advanced industrial societies in the west in the past two decades (Pitts, 1998).

Policing policy

Since the mid-1990s any serious discussion of policing policy in the UK has had to take account of 'zero tolerance'. The idea of zero tolerance is rooted in the analysis of crime control published by George Kelling and James Q. Wilson in their *Atlantic Monthly* article, 'Broken Windows', in 1982. 'The essence of "Broken Windows" is that minor incivilities (such as drunkenness, begging, vandalism, disorderly behaviour, graffiti, litter, etc.), if unchecked and uncontrolled, produce an atmosphere in the community or on a street in which more serious crime will flourish' (Pollard, 1997, p. 46).

The solutions which flow from this analysis involve what Pollard (1997) describes as aggressive, uncompromising law enforcement. This strategy was adopted most famously by William Bratton, erstwhile police chief of New York City, who presided over a 37 per cent drop in crime in general and a 50 per cent drop in the homicide rate between 1994 and 1997 (Bratton, 1997). However, as Jock Young (1998) has observed, similar reductions were achieved in San Diego and other US cities using methods which we in the UK would recognise as 'community' or 'problem-solving' policing, based upon partnerships with local agencies, businesses and citizen groups

(Marlow and Pitts, 1998). The term 'zero tolerance' gained considerable currency in government in the run-up to, and the immediate aftermath of, the 1997 general election and the Home Secretary, Jack Straw, and Prime Minister, Anthony Blair, have both declared themselves to be in favour of it. This is the more perplexing when its alleged author, William Bratton, not only claims never to have used the phrase but, on a recent visit, observed that, in terms of crime, the UK appeared to be a very tranquil place (Young, 1998). Thus far, the only place in the UK which has adopted what is assumed to be a thoroughgoing, New York style, zero-tolerance strategy is Hartlepool, where the results, and what they mean, remain a matter of contention. However, in his address to the Labour Party annual conference in September 1998, Anthony Blair put his weight behind 'zero tolerance' by announcing 25 'crime hotspots' which would be the targets of zero tolerance-style 'order maintenance' interventions.

Secondary prevention

Selective interventions

The evidence from the USA, the UK and mainland Europe all indicates that effective secondary prevention is based upon the careful identification of the groups and the problems to which any proposed intervention is the intended solution (Graham and Bennett, 1995). When this is done the impact of such initiatives on crime, unemployment, depression, drug taking and economic development has sometimes been dramatic (King, 1989; Wiles, 1996; Pitts, 1997, 1998). It would follow therefore that, in this era of burgeoning information technology, agencies concerned with the problem of youth crime should consider developing some form of Geographical Information System (GIS), which enables them to identify the location of the phenomena which appear to be closely associated with youth crime (Hirschfield and Bowers, 1998). Such a system could record:

- incidents of domestic violence to which the police have been called,

- children on the child protection register,
- children received into the care of or 'looked after' by the local authority,
- families involved with the Education Social Work Service as a result of persistent non-attendance,
- people referred to hospital for depression,
- incidents of violent crime and the victims of violent crime,
- racist/racial incidents,
- drug, alcohol and substance abuse incidents,
- youth riots,
- the places from which young runaways run away,
- children and young people who have attempted, or have succeeded in committing, suicide,
- children formally excluded from school,
- young people formally processed by the police,
- rates of population change in neighbourhoods, and
- information on the local economy, family incomes and labour market segmentation.

Analysis of these data would enable agencies to pinpoint neighbourhoods in which many of the factors associated with the commission of criminal and violent acts by young people are most prevalent. This would allow individual agencies to target their work more effectively but the potential of such targetting far greater. This information could, for example, be circulated to the heads of all the relevant local authority and central government services, the police and the voluntary sector, who would constitute a Youth Crime Information Users Group. When devising their annual budgets, the heads of all of these services could be required to indicate how their budgets would be used to alleviate the problems identified by the GIS data, and how their contribution would articulate with the other agencies and organisations to produce a coherent, costed, inter-agency strategy.

Neighbourhood-based youth work

The most comprehensive piece of detached (street) youth work ever undertaken in the UK was the Wincroft Youth Project which operated in Manchester in the late 1960s (Smith *et al.*, 1972). Wincroft utilised techniques developed originally by the New York City Youth Board to deal with several hundred young people, identified by the police, social services, the probation services, schools and youth clubs as posing particular problems of behaviour and criminality. Wincroft worked with these young people in their peer groups over a three-year period. Broadly the project offered young people a wider range of roles that they might play and alternative paths to adulthood. The project proved to be effective in engaging 'hard-to-reach' young people and enabling them either to stop offending or to reduce the frequency and seriousness of their offending. Recently similar 'social education' (pedagogical) methods have been developed in the Initiative Against Aggression and Violence in the new *Länder* in Germany in the late 1980s and 1990s (Bohn, 1996) and the French Social Prevention Initiative. In France, most urban neighbourhoods have youth service-sponsored crime prevention teams, composed of social workers and youth workers who have no formal links with, or accountability to, the justice system. They undertake an analysis of local patterns of youth crime, violence and disorder and the location of young people believed to be at risk in a variety of ways. On the basis of this analysis, certain neighbourhoods or groups are identified for intervention. One team in Paris identified a group of young drug users, hanging around the bus station. The agency gave the team 18 months in which to establish relationships with the target group, and up to five years to locate and work with a broader network of around 300 drug-abusing young people in that part of the city. The work involved individual and small group counselling, introductions to detoxification centres, and drug programmes, introductions to work and training, advocacy with the police, courts and families and help in starting small businesses (King, 1989; De Liege, 1989; Picard, 1995; Pitts, 1998). These initiatives appear to have had a considerable impact upon the nature and intensity of youth offending and there are indications that project participants tend to 'grow out of crime' at an earlier stage than non-participants.

The prototype for all these forms of neighbourhood-based youth work was the Chicago Area Project (CAP) which began in the mid-1930s. In their 50-year follow-up study, Samuel Schlossman and his associates (1984) concluded that the evidence 'while hardly foolproof, justifies a strong hypothesis that CAP has long been effective in reducing rates of reported delinquency'. Despite the fact that the youth service in general and 'detached' or 'street' youth work in particular has been contracting for the past two decades, there is still potential for developing these types of interventions in the UK (see Williamson, 1995). In 1993 the Department for Education and Employment launched its three-year GEST programme for the youth service, the Youth Action Scheme. The scheme supported 28 English local authorities to create 60 projects which aimed to enable youth workers to develop new ways of working which would reduce the risk of young people becoming involved in crime. These projects aimed to:

- develop problem-focused approaches,
- set up time-limited work with young people,
- develop a monitoring and evaluation strategy,
- establish structures to enable short-term financial management, and
- develop an exit strategy.

An evaluation undertaken by Alan France and Paul Wiles (1996) indicates that projects which accepted a crime-focused role were largely successful in developing new ways of working with young-sters in trouble. In their first year, Youth Action Scheme projects worked with 4322 young people, most of whom were demonstrably at risk, or already involved in criminal activity. Despite problems of implementation and evaluation, it appears that these projects had a positive impact upon participants' involvement in crime. This is the more remarkable when we recognise that the bulk of them would have been unlikely to engage in conventional rehabilitative programmes.

Medium-term youth work strategies of this kind are increasingly difficult to fund in the UK and this is unfortunate for a number of reasons. Not least of these is that, as Elliott *et al.* (1986) have shown, 84 per cent of the serious violent offenders interviewed in the US National Youth Survey had no arrest record. Only an effective neighbourhood-based youth programme would be able to make and sustain contact with, and exert some influence over, these young people who are currently in touch with nobody who can contain their behaviour.

Jobs, training and education

Utilising data generated by Geographical Information Systems, local economic development strategies, aimed specifically at multiply deprived, high crime neighbourhoods, and aiming to reconnect the adults and young people in them with the local economy, can be devised. Such strategies strive to attract and support inward investment and new businesses while developing complementary, neighbourhood-based youth and adult training programmes, and expanding access to Further Education and actual and virtual universities (like the Open University) for local people. Characteristically, seed funding for such initiatives is sought via the government's Single Regeneration Budget programme, EU economic development funds, or the UK's own stupidity tax, aka the National Lottery).

Neighbourhood action

Evidence from New York, Paris and London suggests that neighbourhoods with high levels of crime and violence have the lowest levels of social and political participation, and that those neighbourhoods which organise politically have much lower levels of crime, violence and harassment (McGahey, 1986; Pitts, 1998). 'Community' or 'neighbourhood' workers in such neighbourhoods work with residents in order that they may become effective political constituencies, able to articulate their problems, needs and demands to one another and the local and central government politicians and agencies with formal responsibility for community safety and crime control. In Mills' (1957) phrase, the neighbourhood worker's job is to transform 'private troubles' into 'public issues'. However it is important that the attempt to engage the hard-pressed residents of high crime neighbourhoods in the political process does not become confused with the idea that the crime to which they are subject is simply their problem and one which they alone should solve. Such an approach to 'partnership' is at least unjust and, given that the factors which generate this crime are largely beyond the control of local people, none too clever either.

Child protection

In their longitudinal study of young offenders, Farrington and West (1993) found that pre-natal injury and substance abuse were linked with low birth weight which, in turn, was linked with poor school attainment, 'anti-social behaviour', substance abuse, 'hyperactivity', low IQ scores and speech disorders. If parents were young, single and poor when the child was five, he or she was more likely to be convicted as a juvenile. The presence of a father appeared to ameliorate these effects, not least, one suspects, because it tended to boost family income, thus avoiding many of the perils described above, all of which are closely associated with poverty. The Cambridge Study of Delinquent Development also found that 'harsh or erratic parental discipline, cruel, passive or neglecting parental attitude, poor supervision and parental conflict, measured at age eight, all predicted later convictions'. Harsh discipline at eight also 'predicted' future violent offending. The study therefore concludes that aggressive and violent behaviour is transmitted from generation to generation.

As we have noted, although domestic violence and child abuse occur throughout the social structure, recent scholarship (Messerschmidt, 1993; Segal, 1990; Campbell, 1993) suggests that, rather than being randomly distributed, violence against women and children tends to be concentrated amongst the poorest families in the poorest neighbourhoods (Segal, 1990). It is also evident that children who experience or observe adult violence in their formative years are far more likely to go on to perpetrate violence themselves (cf. Howell *et al.*, 1995). What is obviously, and urgently, needed therefore is a thoroughgoing *child protection system* rather than the *child rescue* service which currently goes by that name in the UK. What is required is a well-resourced and flexible service which is able to support families to deal with the real-life stresses which they encounter from day to day in their neighbourhoods (Cooper *et al.*, 1995). Elliott Currie, the American criminologist (1991), argues that these services must offer opportunity-oriented, rather than the more usual and far cheaper, deficit-oriented programmes: 'changed lives' rather than the reluctant compliance with the demands of officialdom, which is the hallmark of so much current child protection work.

Conclusion

The rediscovery of prevention could usher in an era of imaginative innovation in which local and central government, statutory and voluntary agencies, the business community and the residents of high crime neighbourhoods and their children get together to make the world a safer place.

For youth justice and crime prevention agencies, 'prevention' could usher in a period of expansion, and a central place in the corporate community safety strategies which New Labour is requiring local authorities to develop. For professionals, the reappearance of 'prevention' as a legitimate area of endeavour holds the promise that a broader repertoire of professional skills will be required of them than in the 1980s, when what Elliott Currie has called minimalist 'systems management' strategies reigned supreme. However New Labour appears to be unwilling to countenance 'social' solutions to social problems, and eager to demonstrate that they are 'tough on the causes of crime', and so a strategy which identifies lack of self-control as the problem, and focuses on the child-rearing practices of young lone parents, and the class control techniques of young school teachers, has come to the fore.

The danger is that these developments will abet the entrepreneurism of some agencies and the aspirations of some professionals, while leaving the origins of youth crime untouched. While it is obvious that the proclivities of individuals play a significant role in the problem of crime, it is also clear that crime is not reducible to the inability of some parents to instil a capacity for self-control in their children; yet these are the tacit assumptions which are informing current developments. Professionals have a right and a duty to resist this illogical narrowing of their perspective.

An effective preventive strategy requires the active collaboration of a variety of statutory and voluntary agencies and the police, and must be monitored and evaluated rigorously in order to keep it on target. For that reason, participants must be committed to shared goals, shared methods of data collection and the development and modification of professional and administrative practices as the strategy develops over time. Much of the research on inter-agency collaboration in the sphere of crime prevention points to the fact that 'partnership' is not enough and that it is the development of shared experience and the development of a shared 'culture' which determines the effectiveness of such partnerships. This research also suggests that the active support and commitment of key figures at the head of the participating agencies is essential if they are to be more than talking shops in which agencies simply attempt to discharge or displace their own agency responsibilities, or forums in which the most powerful agency attempts to subordinate the others to its will.

8

Preventive Work in Schools

Schools are where children and young people are supposed to spend a great many of their waking hours. As such, the school should be an ideal location for preventing youth offending. Schools are also places where a great deal of victimisation starts, and intervening in schools allows us to address both offending and victimisation simultaneously. Beyond this, of course, unlike the youth court or the offices of the youth offending team which are by their nature 'exclusionary', and hence stigmatising, schools are a mainstream, 'normal', and hence non-stigmatising, service.

School-based early years prevention

Pre-school and early years school programmes appear to reduce crime in general and violent crime in particular. The Perry Pre-School Program in the USA (Farrington, 1996) and the Swedish strategy which aims to give the children of economic migrants a 'flying start' in the educational system, appear to reduce subsequent criminal involvement significantly. In the Perry Pre-School Program, conducted in an African-American neighbourhood in Michigan, pre-school children attended a centre each day for two years and were visited weekly by the staff. The children followed a 'plan–do–review' programme which maximised intellectual stimulation and fostered reasoning powers. Curiously, the gains in measured intelligence were not 'sustained' after the programme closed, raising fascinating questions about whether, and to what extent, intelligence is shaped by social and environmental factors. The experiment also revealed that motivation and behaviour at elementary school were better for programme participants than for the control group. At 19, programme participants were more likely to have graduated from high school and at 27 the programme group had accumulated half as many arrests as the controls. Whatever else the Perry Pre-School Program illustrates, it appears to be telling us that, if we devote the time, attention and educational resources to socially deprived families which middle-class families take for granted, their children will achieve middle-class success goals. In a rational world this finding would be political dynamite. Why the Perry Pre-School Program succeeded is disputed. For Farrington (1996) it is because participants were equipped with the conceptual skills to think through the consequences of crime. It seems more likely, however, that, by giving these children an educational 'head start' in their early years, the programme handed them both the confidence and the tools with which to make their way out of the 'ghetto' into the socioeconomic mainstream where crime and violence as problem-solving devices are less effective. Experience in the UK also shows that vulnerable children from fragile families who have difficulty in making the transition from home to school and from primary school to secondary school, and those who begin to drift away from the school and into violent crime around the ages of 14 and 15 appear to benefit from intensive support.

Anti-bullying strategies

Early work by Power *et al.* (1972) and Rutter *et al.* (1978) indicates that the structure and ethos of schools can have a significant impact upon attendance, attainment, behaviour in class, levels of bullying and students' involvement in crime. A number of recent initiatives in UK secondary schools have endeavoured to improve participation by students, enhance their study skills, increase teachers' competence and cultivate pride in the school, and these have led to decreases in 'self-report delinquency'. Similarly 'whole school' anti-bullying initiatives like the one outlined in Table 8.1 below have been shown to reduce violence both in schools and in the catchment areas around schools (Graham, 1988; Olweus, 1989; Pitts and Smith, 1995). We also know that, in high crime neighbourhoods, behaviour in and out of school is closely linked and that effective intervention in the school to improve communication, clarify expectations, identify rewards and sanctions and offer training and support to staff and students to effect change can have a marked effect upon youth violence (Graham, 1988).

Working with Young Offenders

Table 8.1   Whole school anti-bullying programmes

General prerequisites
1. Awareness of the problem
2. Involvement in devising solutions

Measures at school level
1. Questionnaire survey
2. Structured school-wide discussion of bully/victim problems
3. Improved supervision/surveillance of play areas during breaks
4. More attractive play areas/broader range of break activities
5. Confidential contact for victims and others concerning bullying
6. Meetings about bullying between staff and parents
7. Teacher working parties on strategies for developing positive social
    relationships between students

Measures at class level
1. Class rules against bullying: clarification of proscribed behaviour, praise for
    non-bullying behaviour and the development of realistic and mutually agreed
    sanctions
2. Regular class meetings
3. Role-playing and using literature which highlights the plight of scapegoated
    groups and individuals
4. Encouraging co-operative, as opposed to competitive, learning
5. Shared positive class activities, trips, parties, and so on

Measures at individual level
1. Formal confrontation of students who bully
2. Formal meetings with students' parents
3. Encouragement of 'neutral' students to help
4. Encouragement of parents to help, through production of information folders,
    contact telephone numbers, and so on
5. Organising discussion groups for parents of students who bully or are bullied
6. Devising clear and quick procedures for a change of class or school, should
    this prove necessary

Some whole school anti-bullying initiatives draw upon an 'organisational development' approach which proceeds from the assumption that the policy objectives of complex 'human service' organisations are most likely to be realised if they win the support, and articulate the interests, of members of that organisation at all levels (Pitts and Smith, 1995). This support is gained by a process of continuous consultation and it is this process which holds the key to the success of such approaches. As Diana Robbins (1989) suggests, the most important aspect of the development of policy and strategy in these situations will often be the impact that the process of their formulation has on the culture and ethos of the organisation.

In a similar vein, Olweus (1989), like many other theorists, practitioners and commentators on interpersonal behaviour in schools, suggests that structure, culture and patterns of communication have a significant impact on the conduct of students (Hargreaves, 1967; Power *et al.*, 1972; Willis, 1977; Rutter *et al.*, 1978). Thus effective interventions are concerned, not merely to generate new rules or programmes aimed at the modification of individual behaviour, but with organisational changes which have an impact upon school culture. The key elements in this process are the facilitation of communication between all members of the school community and the harnessing of their collective resources in combating bullying and violence. While good communication and co-operation are central features of any organisational task, they are particularly pertinent to an anti-bullying campaign. Bullying thrives in an atmosphere of secrecy; victims and bystanders fear reprisals if they report a bullying incident; without knowledge of the incident, staff cannot intervene to protect the victim and, accordingly, they are not seen by young people as an effective source of help to which they can turn. All members of the school community can easily become trapped in this cycle and become resigned to their powerlessness. It is therefore important to institute consultative exercises which enable members at all levels of the school to participate in the analysis of the problem, and the construction of a collective response to it. In this way the strategies which emerge are relevant to the particular circumstances of the school concerned and, importantly, all members of the school community can experience 'ownership' of the endeavour.

An 'organisational development' approach can offer a way of identifying and working with those features of the school which promote, or inhibit, violent victimisation. The literature on the development and operation of violent sub-cultures in prisons and residential establishments (Mathiesen, 1964; Jones, 1968; Millham *et al.*, 1978; Rutter and Giller, 1983; Dennington and Pitts, 1991) suggests that bullying and violent victimisation are most likely to occur in settings where

- there is an extensive and rigid hierarchy in which information flow from those at the bottom to those at the top of the hierarchy is poor;

- individual members of staff, who are the organisation's culture carriers, pursue incompatible goals and espouse or enact conflicting values;
- the deployment of rewards and punishments appears to be arbitrary and done without reference to a common standard or set of rules;
- staff appear to be indifferent to violent behaviour not directed at themselves;
- there is no expression of warmth between people at different levels of the organisation.

Conversely bullying and violent victimisation will be least likely to occur in an organisation where

- there is a relatively flat hierarchy in which information flow upwards and downwards is maximised and where that information affects decisions made by staff;
- staff, in consultation with other members of the organisation, have regular opportunities to discuss goals and values and participate in policy formulation;
- the deployment of rewards and punishments is seen to be fair and proportional and corresponds to standards or rules to which members of the organisation at all levels can subscribe;
- staff are actively concerned about violent behaviour; and
- there are frequent, spontaneous expressions of warmth between people at different levels of the hierarchy.

The goal of organisational development is to facilitate the movement of the organisation along the continuum, from the former type of organisational structure towards the latter. While bullying, and other anti-social behaviour in schools, do not simply originate within the school, research suggests that the structure of a school, and the culture it generates, can either contain and reduce, or exacerbate, such behaviour (Hargreaves, 1967; Power *et al.*, 1972; Rutter *et al.*, 1978).

Preventive work in schools in high crime neighbourhoods

As with whole school anti-bullying initiatives, in addition to focusing on vulnerable children and young people in and out of school, the school itself may become the target for interventions which strive to reduce both youth crime and youth victimisation. This may be a particularly useful strategy in high crime neighbourhoods.

State schools have been under pressure since the 1970s. However cuts in education budgets, demographic change and the fragmentation of the large urban education authorities, which were sometimes able to 'engineer' the social and economic mix of secondary schools, have meant that many of the relatively successful comprehensive schools in poorer neighbourhoods of the 1970s have been transformed into the 'failing' schools of the 1990s. A recent study of 15 schools, identified by OFSTED (Office of Standards in Education) as 'failing', revealed that they were all serving communities with high levels of youth crime, social deprivation and unemployment, a high proportion of single-parent families and a high uptake of free school meals (Centre for Educational Management, 1997). The report notes that these schools tended to have poor premises and that their intake represented the residuum of children that selective secondary schools had rejected. Many of the schools in the sample had recently amalgamated or reorganised in the face of demographic change and local competition.

The reasons for such 'failure' are complex. In a study of student–student violence in a school in East London (Pitts and Smith, 1995), it was evident that, with the introduction of local management of schools (LMS) and real cuts in school budgets, school governors faced increasing difficulties in maintaining pastoral services for the growing numbers of socially disadvantaged students entering the school. This increase is attributable, in some degree, to the wholesale deinstitutionalisation of children and young people in need and in trouble since the late 1970s. As Table 8.2 indicates, between 1977 and 1996/8 the numbers of children and young people in residential or custodial institutions, or attending off-site educational or daycare units, fell from around 66 000 to 27 000. However welcome these developments may have been on humanitarian grounds, they meant that mainstream education was confronted by a substantially increased number of abused and/or neglected children and young people with serious behavioural problems, who in a previous era would have been dealt with outside the educational mainstream, and few, if any, additional resources with which to fashion a response.

Table 8.2   Changes in the numbers of children and young people
educated/contained outside mainstream provision

	1977	1996/8
Children's homes	25 000	7 000[1]
Approved schools/Community homes &	6 003	750
Children's homes with education	—	375[2]
Borstal/young offender institutions	8 625	6 615[3]
Boarders in special schools	21 184	9 784[4]
Education. Department behavioural units/Pupil referral units	3 962 (*F/T*)	3 244[5] (*P/T 5–15 hrs*)
Intermediate treatment centres	1 500 (*F/T*)	0[6]
Total	66 274	27 153

Note: *F/T* = free time; *P/T* = past time.
Sources:
[1] Berridge, D. (1998) *Children's Homes Revisited*, Jessica Kingsley.
[2] DHSS (1975) 'Young Offenders in Care, Preliminary Report' (unpublished); DHSS (1978) 'Preliminary Report on Care Order Survey' (unpublished); DoH (1996) *Annual Return* Education Prevision in. CHEs.
[3] *Prison Statistics* (1977) HMSO; Millham, S. *et al.* (1978) *Locking Up Children*, Saxon House.
[4] DfEE (June 1998) unpublished statistics.
[5] Her Majesty's Inspectors of Schools (1978) *Behavioural Units*; DoE, DfEE (1996) *Survey of LEAs* (101 of 109).
[6] DHSS (1978) Survey of Local Authority Social Services Departments (unpublished).

It is against the backdrop of neighbourhood destabilisation, dein-stitutionalisation and the pressures placed upon schools by the national school league tables that the rise in school exclusion must be understood. Between 1991–2 and 1993–4, formal permanent and fixed-term exclusions from schools in England and Wales rose from 2910 to 3833. By 1997, permanent exclusions stood at 13 500 and fixed-term exclusions at 135 000. In the late 1990s, 70–80 per cent of permanent exclusions involved 14–16-year-old male pupils. Boys outnumbered girls by at least 4 to 1 (21 to 1 in primary schools). School exclusion is closely associated with abuse, neglect and family disruption. Black Afro-Caribbean students are excluded at six times the rate of white students.

There is evidence of a link between exclusion and offending. *Misspent Youth* found that 42 per cent of offenders of school age who are sentenced in the youth court have been excluded from school (Audit Commission, 1996). The Home Office survey of young people aged between 14 and 25 found a strong relationship between both temporary and permanent exclusion and offending. Of the 11 per cent of males in their sample who had been excluded on a fixed-term basis, three-quarters had offended. Of those females who had been temporarily excluded – 4 per cent of the sample – half were offenders. Though numbers were small, this relationship was even stronger in regard to young people permanently excluded from school (Graham and Bowling, 1995). There is also evidence that the exclusion itself can lead to further offending. In one local authority, 58 per cent of children aged 11 or more who were permanently excluded offended either in the year before or the year after exclusion. However this group was known to commit 50 per cent more offences in the year after the exclusion had taken place (Audit Commission, 1996). The Audit Commission argues that the excluded group, while relatively small, contains some of the most persistent offenders. A study of the costs of exclusion also found that the cases of approximately a quarter of excluded pupils result in costs to the police, and indeed that costs to the police and criminal justice services form over 70 per cent of the total costs of agencies other than education. It would follow from this that any school-based intervention which managed to reduce the levels of school exclusion would have significant benefits for a whole range of agencies and individuals, not least the young people themselves.

In a recent study of student victimisation in a mixed secondary school in London (Porteous, 1998) the transience of those living on the public housing estates, which constituted the school's catchment area, was reflected in a 50 per cent turnover in the school roll between years 7 and 11 (30 per cent of year 10 – 14–15-year-olds – and 64 per cent of year 11 – 15–16-year-olds – had previously attended another secondary school). Because the nature of the changes in the neighbourhood had been to replace more prosperous residents with less prosperous ones, by 1997 over 50 per cent of school students qualified for free school meals, indicating that their parent(s) were in receipt of state benefits. Poverty and transience generate educational disadvantage in children, and erode the capacity of adults to offer consistent parenting. Thus the school must absorb a higher proportion of children with special educational and behavioural needs. Indeed, in 1997, 44 per cent of the school's students were the subjects of, or in the process of assessment for, a 'statement of special educational needs', twice the borough average. As a result, behaviour in the school playground and the corridors had deteriorated. The impact of the resultant atmosphere could be measured in increased truancy and lateness amongst students who were previously seen to pose no particular problems.

A further consequence of rapid student turnover is that such schools have a large number of vacancies. In the current economic climate, in which local education authorities are striving to reduce surplus capacity, these schools are under constant pressure to absorb students who wish to transfer into them. Beyond the destabilising impact of this steady influx of new students upon established peer groups, and the student's informal 'pecking order', is the fact that many of them bring additional academic and behavioural problems with them. It is, of course, ironic that schools in 'destabilised neighbourhoods', confronting the formidable effects of social problems, are, nonetheless, required to accept a disproportionate number of older adolescents, many of whom are transferring as a result of exclusion or conflict in their previous school.

In the school in question, between September 1996 and April 1997, 41 per cent of year 11 students were assaulted, with 30 per cent of these assaults occurring in the vicinity of the school or on the way home from school, in the hour or so following the end of the school day. Of the perpetrators, 80 per cent were male, and 48 per cent were described as being either strangers or students from another school; 24 per cent of respondents reported being threatened or assaulted with a weapon. David Porteous (1998) notes:

> Many more pupils from ethnic minorities reported that they had experienced racist abuse or violence, 35 per cent of all 'non-white' respondents compared to 16 per cent of whites. Asian pupils, 46% of whom said they had experienced racism, seem particularly vulnerable. They were more likely than any other ethnic group to have been threatened with violence and to have been hit or kicked or pushed about.

Seeing 'the writing on the wall', some parents transfer their children to other schools, further destabilising the school they leave. This has the effect of reducing the proportion of parents who have made a positive choice in favour of the school, and increasing the proportion who are unwilling, or unable, to make a choice about their child's education. These were not simply neglectful parents. Some of them, like the refugees from Eritrea, Ethiopia or Bosnia, speak little English and have been traumatised by the experience of violence, change and loss. The parents who seek a transfer tend to be more prosperous and articulate and are often active in fund-raising efforts and the PTA. They are also the parents who are most likely to reinforce the school's espoused ethos at home. Their departure is a double blow for the school, diminishing both the material and moral resources crucial to the development of its 'social capital'. It was also found that, whereas most 'failing schools' were serving students from areas with a high level of deprivation, 'better off' students were increasingly congregating in other, better-resourced schools.

Staff morale

Not surprisingly, these changes tend to undermine staff morale, and so the problems in the student group are mirrored in staff absenteeism and a rapid turnover of teachers. As a result, destabilised schools usually carry a higher proportion of probationary teachers, supply teachers and, as a result of the transfer of teacher education to the schools in the early 1990s, student teachers. This is particularly ironic since all the teachers interviewed in the study reported above agreed that their students do not like 'new faces', take time to trust people and need to gain experience in forming positive relationships with adults.

The changes afflicting these schools have, of course, been paralleled by the introduction of the national curriculum, school performance league tables, the Conservatives' 'local management of schools' initiative, real cuts in funding, serious reductions in the education social work service, school counselling, pastoral care, home–school liaison, home tuition, off-site units, child and family guidance clinics, the youth service and those non-governmental welfare and youth-serving agencies not undertaking statutory youth justice and child protection work. These changes have eroded the ability of these schools to deal with the problems presented by their students. In parallel, the additional work generated for teachers by 'problem students'; meetings with students, their parents, social welfare and criminal justice agencies, the production of reports for, and attendance at, case conferences, court hearings and so on, has burgeoned.

In this situation, many teachers feel that the ethos of the school is being engulfed by the alternative ethos of 'the street', and they no longer feel in control. One of the consequences of this is that they become less willing to deal with hostile and aggressive behaviour from students. This means that senior staff come to assume increasing responsibility for behavioural matters and 'difficult classes'. But this compounds the problem, since the more disruptive or aggressive students perceive the effective withdrawal from such confrontations as a capitulation by junior staff. Feeling disempowered to deal with incidents individually, staff become more willing to involve their trade unions. Thus, relatively minor instances of violence or verbal abuse may become a 'union matter', with the result that the offending child may be excluded from the school by senior staff in order to avert industrial action. Ironically, of course, this serves to undermine the authority of both junior and senior staff in the eyes of students even more. As Menzies Lyth (1960) has observed, in situations of great uncertainty and anxiety, professionals will fall back upon structures and protocols to assuage those anxieties. This tendency is evident in the progressive bureaucratisation of interactions between senior staff and junior staff, and staff and students in hard-pressed schools.

Paradoxically, the current tendency on the part of local education authorities to respond to these problems by sending in a 'behavioural task force' has the potential to make the problems, described above, worse, further destabilising an already destabilised school. Staff and students interviewed are agreed that such task forces send an unequivocal message that 'The staff can't 'cut it' so they've had to send for the "A Team"'.

Constructing an inter-agency intervention

Presented below are some vignettes from the strategy devised by a multi-agency group (teachers, governors, a voluntary youth serving agency, the youth service, the chief executives department, the youth justice service, the educational social work service, the police and a university research team) to combat the problems of violence and victimisation in the school described above. They observed that:

- Urgent action is needed on inward transfers if the school is to 'stabilise'. This will require a policy shift by the education committee. (Head to pursue with inspectors, governor to pursue with councillors.)
- The stability of the staff group is central to the stability of the school and incentives and supports should be devised to help achieve this goal. These would include the participative development of whole school strategies and possibly some consultancy/professional supervision by an external facilitator or facilitators.
- The school should use local voluntary sector agencies to support staff in the development of appropriate large and small group skills, assertiveness and confrontation.
- Mentoring schemes during the primary/secondary transition may be crucial to enable some children to be 'contained' within the school and the school should seek funds to establish them.
- The school should initiate small group *personal relationships* schemes which give high levels of personal attention to older students who are becoming marginal to the school and/or experiencing problems at home or in the community. They may also constitute a Caution+ (*final warning* scheme) option which would serve as a 'normalising' and integrative, as opposed to a stigmatising and exclusionary, response to offending.
- The school should establish a staff–student *personal safety working party* as a sub-committee of the governors, reporting to them. This group should meet regularly with their local councillor and the local authority Community Safety Strategy Group to discuss how their efforts in the school and neighbourhood are articulating with the broader strategy.
- The school should create informal spaces where staff and students can 'just talk'.
- The school should create safe, staffed, places inside the building at breaks, possibly involving youth workers and volunteers, with special spaces for Muslim girls only.
- The school should institute a Bully Box system, in which students can place a note asking to speak to the member of staff of their choice in confidence.

- The school should institute a Student Mentoring System.
- The school should breathe new life into the School Council.
- The school should promote the consistent representation of the interests of children and young people as victims rather than perpetrators of crime in borough fora where decisions about community safety are made.
- The school should create women's groups for female students (maybe using volunteers).
- The school should create positive men's groups for male students which focus particularly on the changing role of men and explore how a plausible male identity can be sustained without recourse to violence (maybe using volunteers).
- The school should tackle staff bullying and racism and suspend staff if necessary.
- The school should institute systems of staff support and consultancy which focus upon staff anxieties, the development of support systems and the continuing control, by staff, of the in-school behaviour of students. Staff need to feel that they are heard and that they will be protected: training, liaison and discussion with local police on a mechanism for handling threats from parents and siblings are necessary.
- The school should appoint ex-students as teachers' aides and recreational counsellors to work with the students in classes, in breaks and after school. In many French schools this served to reduce after-school victimisation dramatically.
- After-school clubs and local youth work initiatives should be timed in such a way that students will be making their journey home at different times and via different routes. This can be another way of disrupting patterns of victimisation.
- In neighbourhoods like this, parent–teacher associations (PTAs) tend not to work very well. We understand that in some of the French banlieues the *Femmes Relais*, a group of non-white French mothers brought together by North African animateurs from the mayor's office, came to discharge this PTA function very effectively. This group regularly met local politicians, senior personnel from the schools, the police and the recreational, health and welfare services to discuss questions of educational attainment, truancy, bullying, racism, drugs and so on. As a significant and independent local political constituency, they had an important impact upon policy. Single Regeneration Budget money is available to develop work with parents in the neighbourhood and

Adult Education anthorities are keen to develop a joint project with the school along these lines.

- Vocational training should be long-term and progressive, enabling participants to eventually acquire the qualifications/ experience to enter primary sector employment outside the area. To this end one of the deputy heads is liaising with the local employment services head to devise more extensive vocational programmes for some of the students who are rejecting the more academic elements of the curriculum. This training should be linked closely with the school and this means that it should prob- ably start while the student is at school since, as Sullivan (1989), argues, schools run far more smoothly, and are far more tranquil places, when students perceive the school as a stepping stone to, and a source of, status-conferring vocational opportunity.

Student perspectives

In a survey and subsequent 'focus groups', students expressed concern about the following areas.

Racism

- Racism is understood by students as prejudice against someone else because of their colour and culture, but there is no sense amongst many white students that, for minority groups, racism means more than being on the receiving end of verbal or physi- cal abuse.
- The majority of older students recognise that Asian students do experience a great deal of racism in the school but argue that this is self-imposed – that they 'ask for it'.
- Asian students are said by white and Afro-Caribbean students to be very different because of their clothes and their language. This is somewhat ironic since the bulk of the Asian students at the school share a similar style of dress and, in many cases, a similar accent with their white and Afro-Caribbean counterparts.
- The prevalent view amongst white and Afro-Caribbean students is that Asian students 'give it back', that is retaliate very readily. However, the survey data on violent victimisation suggest that the bulk of racist incidents or racially inspired conflict is initiated

by white students. Older Asian students recognise this to be the case.

Observations

- Wherever possible, it would be desirable to keep together the mixed race peer groups which form in primary school. Many teachers argue that the preservation of these bonds is the strongest bulwark against racist conflict.
- Local histories and sociologies can be used to illustrate the origins of local conflicts and to offer a broader, less personalised analysis. This can involve older local residents and/or local history groups. Such work could focus upon the racialisation of this conflict in the recent past and highlight geographical and economic factors and the struggle for limited resources. Such work can also stress the positives of the area and the fact that each of the many groups which have lived there were, originally, newcomers.
- Students feel that questions of racism, sexism, macho culture and violence should be dealt with throughout the curriculum, not simply in reaction to the latest incident.
- Some staff suggest that, in dealing with these issues, drama and the arts are often preferable to more didactic methods since they allow students to place themselves 'in each other's shoes'.
- The 'Personal and Social Education' lessons could be used to look at students' real-life experience of racism and the ways in which they deal with it.

Violence

- Fights between students usually start with cussing and then escalate.
- There is an unwritten code, seemingly shared by all students, that cussing one's family is very serious. Although a large amount of cussing goes on between friends, including racist cussing, it is serious cussing by someone from outside your social group which usually leads to fights.
- This sequence of events often starts in the classroom.
- Many fights between boys are regarded by other students as fairly

trivial and, once the fight is over, boys will often make up quite quickly.

- When girls fight each other, the dispute generally lasts much longer and the conflict may eventually involve a wide network of friends.
- There is a hierarchy of toughness within the school. Older white and Afro-Caribbean students are most likely to be near the top, but it is possible for Asian boys to be there if they are perceived to be able to 'handle themselves'.
- The dominant sub-cultural values in the school are those of the white, working class male majority, some of whom are from 'important' known families with a reputation on the estates in the area.
- As a result, some family disputes are imported into the school. Youth and community workers who have lived in the borough for a long time say that this has been the case for at least the last 25 years.
- White boys in years 10 and 11 say that there is far less conflict and fighting in the upper forms because the 'pecking order' has been sorted out.
- Asian boys, by contrast, say that conflict and fighting is less common in years 7 and 8 but gets worse in years 9, 10 and 11. It seems that, while the fighting between white students decreases, the interracial fighting, particularly outside the school, grows and often involves older adolescents and young adults from beyond the school. This can become particularly dangerous, but some students saw it as exciting and dramatic, making them feel quite important. The streets outside the school are more dangerous places for boys from years 9, 10 and 11, and more so if they are identified as being part of the local white or Asian 'posses'. However there is always the danger of misrecognition and a number of older students have been attacked simply because somebody thought they might have been 'connected' with a posse in this way.

Observations

- The school needs a clear reiteration of school rules and school policy vis-à-vis violence and racism.

- It also needs to be clear when, and under what circumstances, the police will be called into the school.
- Senior staff should explore the reorientation of police patrols to focus upon likely incidents or trouble spots outside the school at key times.
- School staff should reorient their playground duties in accordance with an in-school victimisation survey which identifies 'hot spots', peak times for victimisation and vulnerable groups.
- Delegitimation of targets: there is a need to disrupt patterns of victimisation by mobilising white concern about Asian victimisation and vice versa (cf. Forrester *et al.*, 1990).
- Senior staff should avoid mediation and attempts at restorative justice in cases of violent victimisation. They could make matters worse.
- Close liaison with relevant local agencies through the new Community Safety Strategy Groups to be convened by local authorities under the provisions of the Crime and Disorder Act 1998 will be crucial.

Evaluation: how will it work?

Central to this project is the attempt to learn not only 'what works', if indeed it does, but how, and under what circumstances, it works and whether it is likely to work elswhere without consuming inordinate resources. Such an approach requires the multi-agency team to:

- make explicit their views about the nature of the problems thrown up by the research;
- specify the type and levels of change they wish to achieve in the short, medium and longer term, and the areas in which they wish to achieve them (that is, whether they want or need to work on all the problem areas identified);
- specify the interventions which should be instituted to effect the desired change in the short, medium and longer term;
- specify how the interventions in the short, medium and longer term will affect one another sequentially (that is, elaborate a theory of change?);

- anticipate how measures may interact laterally with one another in the short, medium and longer term;
- anticipate how changes in the environment (new SRB projects, the closure of a local school, the creation of a YOT, and so on) will affect and/or be utilised to develop, the strategy;
- specify the factors which will indicate that change has occurred;
- specify the tools used to measure that change;
- specify the role(s) to be played by each agency, in each part of each strategy;
- specify the resources which will be committed by each agency;
- identify the resources the project must secure beyond those on offer from the participating agencies;
- identify the nature and level of political support/change necessary for the successful implementation of the strategy.

This strategy can, and should, be modified as it proceeds, in the light of the information gathered about its impact. In this way it is possible to discover how the intervention is working rather than merely knowing that it is or is not working, and wondering whether this is a result of anything we did or did not do.

Conclusion

As we have already observed, the effectiveness of school-based programmes can be maximised if the school works closely with relevant local agencies to effect agreed changes. Given the right kind of support, schools in high crime neighbourhoods can act as a bulwark against crime and violence. However, if the effect is to be sustained, the strategy must be continually refreshed by the introduction of new programmes and initiatives. Workers within the youth justice system have tended to be ambivalent about working with schools and, thus far, have had little involvement with the young victims of violent crime. However, with the advent of YOTs, the strong evidence that an assault upon the violent victimisation of young people can have a significant impact upon the perpetration of youth violence in general, could trigger creative interagency work in this area.

9

Preventive Work with Individuals

This chapter considers preventive work with individuals; what is sometimes called 'tertiary' or 'criminality' prevention or rehabilitation. This form of prevention normally focuses upon people who are already involved in crime and it aims to halt, or diminish, this involvement. However, in the mid-1970s, criminologist and practitioners who wanted to engage in primary prevention, or rehabilitation, were faced with a very unpalatable 'fact', for it appeared, as James Q. Wilson (1975) noted, that:

> It does not seem to matter what form of treatment in the correctional system is attempted, whether vocational training or academic education; whether counselling inmates individually, in groups or not at all; whether therapy is administered by social workers or psychiatrists; whether the institutional context of the treatment is custodial or benign; whether the sentences are short or long; whether the person is placed on probation or released on parole; or whether the treatment takes place in the community or in institutions. (Wilson, 1975, p.169)

This sombre assessment, based on Martinson's (1974) survey of 231 research studies, was underscored by many subsequent investigations which drew similarly pessimistic conclusions. Indeed it was on the basis of such evidence that, in the mid-1970s, criminologists reluctantly announced the demise of the 'rehabilitative ideal' (Preston, 1980). Over the next decade or so, a broad consensus emerged to support the view that the best we could hope for in our work with offenders was to minimise the negative impact of prosecution, imprisonment and social work intervention on their lives (Bottoms and McWilliams, 1979; Thorpe *et al.*, 1980; Morris *et al.*,

1980). Although these developments disheartened some criminologists, they offered a ready rationale for the development of the pragmatic 'systems management' strategy, referred to in Chapter 1, which came to dominate professional practice in youth justice in the 1980s.

The rehabilitation of rehabilitation

As we have already noted, as the 1980s advanced, the crime rate rose to record heights, placing more and more political pressure on the government to do something about it. Thus some criminologists and other social scientists, sensing a 'wind of change', returned to the data upon which the belief that 'nothing works' had been based and, not altogether surprisingly, discovered that data now told a rather different story:

> the outcome research of the early 1970s was capable of being interpreted in other ways than 'Nothing works'... This has recently led some writers... who worked at the Home Office Research Unit in the 1970s to argue that the pessimistic conclusions drawn from this research were not necessarily justified. (Blagg and Smith, 1989, p.86)

In this they are no doubt correct, since the 'Nothing Works' doctrine, based as it was on a global analysis of reconviction rates, failed to pinpoint those individuals, projects and institutions whose endeavours did, in fact, 'work'. While such localised data do not undermine the thesis that, in the majority of cases, rehabilitative methods tend not to rehabilitate, they do suggest that sometimes, with some people, in some circumstances, for some reason, some things do 'work'. However this rehabilitation of rehabilitation was palpably political in intent. As Christopher Nutall, described by the *Independent* as the 'hard-headed' director of research and statistics at the Home Office, told a meeting of chief probation officers in 1992: '"Nothing Works" should be killed; not just because it's not right but because it has had a terrible effect. Let's not talk about it any more. Let's talk about what does work.'

The practical consequence of these political manoeuvres was the emergence, in the late 1980s, of the 'justice model' as the rehabilitative model of choice in both adult and youth justice. The justice model was sold to the key political, professional and media constituencies as a tough, confrontational, non-custodial response to offending, aimed at 'high tariff', 'adjudicated offenders' in individualised 'offending programmes', the duration of which was endlessly elastic, determined by the length of the prison sentence to which it was to be an alternative.

The justice model's political fit was vouchsafed by the treatment's obvious remoralising objectives and its claim to address the offender's capacity for moral discernment and rational calculation. As such it served to legitimise the government's attempt to control the spiralling costs of the penal system by reducing the numbers of young offenders going into custody. However this legitimacy could not be achieved by political rhetoric alone. The rehabilitative or correctional techniques had to be shown to be effective or subject to the type of 'objective' evaluation which would, in due course, demonstrate their effectiveness. This opened the door to 'cognitive–behavioural' forms of rehabilitation.

Reasoning and rehabilitation (R&R)

The forms of rehabilitation developed in the 1960s and 1970s aimed to ameliorate the alleged effects of social or emotional deprivation and enable offenders to make 'positive' choices about their lives. The new rehabilitations were, by contrast, concerned to remedy cognitive malfunction in the area of moral choice, to desensitise subjects to 'criminogenic triggers' and eradicate dysfunctional social skills (Ross *et al.*, 1984).

On the basis of a review of the more successful rehabilitative programmes in North America, Robert Ross *et al.* (1984) concluded that those which succeeded in reducing offending generally tried to change the offender's thinking. Of course virtually all rehabilitative programmes aim to change the way young offenders think about crime – who, after all, would fund a project which did not? It is, therefore, unsurprising that two ambitious cognitive psychologists in search of a new and lucrative project should spot this. That they then proceeded to ignore all the other elements of successful programmes in favour of an exclusive focus upon 'Reasoning and

Rehabilitation', as they termed it, is rather more surprising. As to the programme, David Farrington (1996) writes:

> Ross attempted to teach delinquents the cognitive (thinking skills) in which they were deficient, in the expectation that this would lead to a decrease in their offending. His reviews of existing delinquency rehabilitation programmes suggested that those who succeeded in reducing offending generally tried to change the offender's thinking.

Great claims have been made for R&R and its widespread adoption by the probation, prison and youth justice services attests to the fact that these claims have been taken seriously by policy makers and practitioners and underpin many of the orders brought into being by the Crime and Disorder Act (1998). However:

- its claims are based on experiments with jailed adults, not child and adolescent offenders in the community;
- what R&R takes to be a deficit in cognitive functioning may simply be evidence of a different, more 'flexible', value system;
- R&R is based on the erroneous assumption that if one simply thinks 'straight' (logically) then one will necessarily go 'straight' (act lawfully);
- a Netherlands Ministry of Justice survey of youth justice interventions undertaken in the 1980s found R&R and social skills programmes to be no more effective than conventional interventions;
- the research evidence that R&R 'works' is problematic. In the key study, volunteer prisoners were split into a Programme Group and a Waiting List. 28 per cent of the Programme Group did not complete the R&R programme (14 per cent did not start and 14 per cent dropped out or were thrown out for rule breaking, resistance or hostility). Of the remaining Programme Group, 19.7 per cent were reconvicted, against 23 per cent of the Waiting List. However 28 per cent of drop-outs/throw-outs from the Programme Group were reconvicted. Comparing only the Programme 'completers' with the Waiting List, rather than 'completers', 'drop-outs' and 'throw-outs', gives a distorted picture of R&R's impact. Nonetheless reconviction rates amongst non-

Programme and non-Waiting List groups were far higher, leading Pawson and Tilley (1997) to argue that, rather than using these expensive and time-consuming programmes, we should simply place everybody on the waiting list.

Restorative justice (RJ)

The other method of intervention commended by the Crime and Disorder Act (1998) is variously described as mediation, reparation and 'restorative justice' (RJ). The broad contours of restorative justice are described by Mika and Zehr (1997).

- The victims and the community have been harmed and need restoration.
- The primary victims are those most directly affected by the offence but others, such as family members of victims and offenders, witnesses and members of the affected community, are also victims.
- The relationships affected (and reflected) by crime must be addressed.
- Victims, offenders and the affected communities are the key stakeholders in justice.
- A restorative justice process maximises the input and participation of these parties in the search for restoration, healing, responsibility and prevention.
- The state has circumscribed roles, such as investigating facts, facilitating processes and ensuring safety, but the state is not a primary victim.

The most comprehensive study of the impact of RJ has been undertaken in Catalonia. In 1992, Rule 6A (sect. 2) of the Catalonian Penal Code placed victim–offender mediation/ reparation at the heart of the youth justice system (Elejabarrieta *et al.*, 1993; Barberan, 1997). In 1993:

- 40.2 per cent of all cases were dealt with in this way;
- in 68.5 per cent of these cases victims and offenders reached agreement about the remedy;

- in 78.2 per cent of outcomes rated successful, the 'solution' involved 'dialogue' between victim and offender;
- it was hardest to reach agreement in cases with initial 'not guilty' pleas and those involving peer violence;
- it proved easiest to reach agreement in cases of 12- and 13-year-olds involved in 'criminal damage';
- successful outcomes were most frequent in cases involving damage to property and least frequent in cases of interpersonal violence;
- the bulk of victims and offenders participating in the process in Catalonia registered satisfaction (however, there is a tendency for victim satisfaction to fade with time).

The findings in Catalonia are borne out by findings in Northamptonshire and elsewhere in the UK that forms of victim–offender mediation appear to have more relevance and meaning to both victims and offenders. However evidence that they actually stop, or reduce, further offending is far harder to come by. There are a number of reasons for this.

Methodological problems

- Many projects are evaluated too early because of anxieties about funding.
- RJ often constitutes only one element in a diverse programme and it has proved difficult to isolate its specific effects.

Empirical problems

- An analysis of several hundred US RJ programmes indicates high levels of victim–offender satisfaction but negligible impact on reoffending (Howell *et al.*, 1995).

Theoretical problems

- Can young offenders generalise their identification with the victim, in the RJ encounter, to other potential victims? The

Kirkholt study (Forrester *et al.*, 1990) suggests that 'burglars' divide the world into legitimate and illegitimate targets and that, although they 'hate doing it', they do it anyway. Does successful RJ merely serve to delegitimise a particular victim in the mind of the offender rather than develop empathy with all potential victims?

It is not that R&R or RJ do or do not 'work'. Clearly, with some young people in some places, sometimes, these interventions do 'work'. It is more that 'What works?' is not a very helpful question since it is rooted in a whole set of simplistic assumptions about the way correctional programmes and, far more importantly, people work. In opposition to the implicit assumption within R&R that programmes work 'on' individuals, Pawson and Tilley (1997) argue that programmes actually work 'through' individuals. They write:

> Social programs involve a continual round of interactions and opportunities and decisions. Regardless of whether they are born of inspiration or ignorance, the subject's choice at each of these junctures will frame the extent and nature of change. What we are describing here is not just the moment when the subject signs up to enter a program but the entire learning process. The act of volunteering merely marks a moment in a whole evolving pattern of choice. Potential subjects will consider a program (or not), cooperate closely (or not), stay the course (or not), learn lessons (or not), apply the lessons (or not). Each one of these decisions will be internally complex and take its meaning according to the chooser's circumstances.

It follows from this that the effect of rehabilitative programmes will be profoundly affected by the relevance of the programme to the lives of participants. A sophisticated national study conducted in West Germany, which utilised official data collected over the preceding 30 years, found that, in the case of serious and persistent young offenders, probation could be remarkably effective in reducing offending if, within the first 12 weeks of probation the young person was helped to:

- find adequate accommodation,
- organise their finances,

- stabilise their addictions, and
- enter or sustain a relatively secure emotional relationship.

Only then, the researchers argued, can professionals begin to consider their offending.

The Northamptonshire diversion scheme

As we have observed, in the 1980s and early 1990s the orthodoxy in youth justice in England and Wales suggested that, as far as possible, 'low tariff 'offenders should be diverted out of the system and subjected to minimal intervention, while higher tariff offenders should, wherever possible, be dealt with via tightly-focused, time-limited offending programmes in the community. This attempt to minimise intervention stands in marked contrast to the recommendations of the Audit Commission (1996) and the *No More Excuses* White Paper (1997) which advocate robust early intervention aimed at diverting the child or young person from crime rather than the criminal justice system.

It is evident that the thinking of both the Audit Commission and the Home Office policy makers has been shaped by the Northamptonshire Diversion Scheme. The scheme is staffed by seconded workers from the police, social services, probation, the health service and education. As we noted in Chapter 3, the Northants scheme anticipated not only the role, function and constitution of the youth offending teams introduced by the Crime and Disorder Act (1998), but the administrative arrangements under which they will operate and the types of programmes they will run as well. For that reason, it is worth examining the Northants model in some detail.

The Northants Scheme deals with all children and young people apprehended by the police in Northamptonshire, irrespective of the seriousness of the offences for which they are charged. Interestingly, 60 per cent of the cases dealt with by the scheme involve children and young people who are excluded from school. In 1997, 62 per cent of these cases were dealt with by informal warnings, 14 per cent by cautions and 24 per cent by prosecution. The scheme employs 29 workers: police officers, teachers, community psychiatric nurses, mediators, youth workers, youth justice workers and probation officers seconded to the scheme by their agencies for a three-year period. This gives the scheme access to a broad range of professional networks and resources through the agencies of the seconded workers. Workers are accountable in operational matters to the scheme co-ordinator and thence to the scheme management group comprising representatives of all these agencies. In addition the scheme has representation from youth court magistrates, Victim Support and other relevant community groups in order that these groups can gain an awareness of the methods and impact of the scheme, and that their voices can be heard.

All cases referred to the Scheme are discussed by the whole team in order that the proposed intervention accords with the principles of consistency and proportionality. Cases are then referred to one or two workers on the basis of the skills and expertise demanded by the proposed intervention. Workers visit the young person at home to ascertain their views about the offence and what they believe they could do to put matters right. Parents are normally present at this interview. The interview is, in effect, an initial assessment. There may be subsequent visits if the workers deem this to be necessary. Workers then visit the victim(s) to hear their account of the incident, what they feel about it, whether they would be prepared to participate in mediation and what they would consider to be an appropriate remedy. There may be subsequent visits if the workers consider this necessary. The allocated worker(s) then prepare an assessment of the situation, and the young offender, which are taken back to the team for discussion. The team may request further information before agreeing to an intervention. Information about the agreed intervention is then forwarded to the police who, in 76 per cent of the cases, issue a formal warning or a caution, depending upon the seriousness of the offence and other factors outlined above. The worker(s) then return to the victim and the offender to agree the proposed intervention with them. If the victim decides not to go ahead, work can still proceed with a modified programme. If the young offender decides not to go ahead, the case is referred back to the police for further action, which is likely to take the form of a prosecution.

Having undertaken an assessment of both the offence and the young offender, the team may recommend to the police one of the following options.

- No further action
- A formal warning (a formal reprimand from 1998)
- A caution (a final warning from 1998)
- A caution plus
- Prosecution

In the case of a prosecution recommendation being accepted by the police, team members will write a pre-sentence report (see Chapter 5) in which, wherever possible, they will propose a community penalty which accords with the seriousness of the offence, and the skills, abilities and the social and educational needs of the offender (for a fuller account of pre-court diversion, see Chapter 3).

The team's interventions with young people will usually have three foci:

- the offence – this can be resolved by mediation, compensation, reparation or an apology;
- the behaviour – this could involve work on alcohol/drugs, anger management, personal and group relationships, cognitive, psychoanalytic or psychiatric treatment;
- the young person's social situation – this could focus upon parents, schooling, vocational training, work, poverty, housing or leisure.

The emphasis in each of these areas is on building upon the young person's existing strengths.

Impact

The Northants scheme claims to offer a rapid response; all referrals are made within a week, and all programmes are completed within three months. It also claims better reconviction rates (23 per cent over a two-year follow-up period) at one sixth of the costs involved in formally processing a young person through the courts. It is useful to contrast the eclecticism and multiple foci of the Northants scheme with the far more tightly focused and prescriptive methods discussed in the earlier part of this chapter.

Having considered this structure for face-to-face work with young offenders in the justice system, we look in greater detail at the nature of assessment, the types of interventions to which assessment points, the roles and responsibilities of the workers attempting to implement these programmes, both within and beyond the youth justice system and evidence about the impact of these programmes.

Making an assessment

Developing an effective programme for children and young people in trouble is a complex business. From 1999, youth justice workers will be required to develop 'packages' to accompany a police final warning. These packages are intended to act as a sharp deterrent to further involvement in crime and offer some redress to the victim while, at the same time, offering youth justice professionals a means of identifying and working with those factors in the young person's life which are leading them to offend. This particular legislative requirement appears to have been framed on the assumption that criminal careers are constructed out of a series of stepping stones. Thus it is assumed that, if a young person is not dealt with effectively at an early stage in their criminal career, they will proceed to commit crimes of ever greater gravity until they emerge at the other end of the process as a serious and persistent young offender.

In fact, young people's 'criminal careers' unfold in many different ways. Some, particularly in areas characterised by demographic change, acute social need and limited opportunity, do often escalate in this way (McGahey, 1986; Hagan, 1993; Farrington, 1996). However others, like those which involve drug taking by middle class young people or serious violence by young people of all social classes, may well be episodic and short-lived. Pitts (1988), for example, found that the offending careers of black Afro-Caribbean young people tended to start at around 14 or 15 and that, unlike their white counterparts, these youngsters tended to come from families with no previous involvement with the justice system. Some young people will start out stealing small amounts of goods or money when opportunities present themselves and continue to do this for the rest of their lives. As Hagell and Newburn (1994) discovered, it is simply not the case that the bulk of persistent offenders are also serious offenders or vice versa. Importantly it is not at all clear that those young people who eventually become involved in the most serious crimes, murder, rape, aggravated burglary and so on, can be readily identified by an examination of their previous offences or patterns of offending.

This makes the task of assessment particularly difficult. We may well encounter, for example, youngsters whose offences are relatively trivial but whose social situation suggests that they may well be on the threshold of more serious involvement in crime or other self-defeating, self-damaging or dangerous behaviours. Thus, while we may not wish to engage in unnecessary 'net widening', we have a responsibility to address these other factors. The key mechanism whereby both net widening and unduly discretionary, subjective and intuitive decision making can be avoided is an effective system of assessment. There are three main reasons for using formal assessment and classification systems:

- to provide greater validity, structure and consistency to the assessment and the decision-making process,
- to allocate limited resources most effectively by aiming the most intensive interventions at those children and young people most at risk of embarking upon an offending career, and
- to ensure fairness and consistency between the children and young people under consideration by making all decisions in accordance with the same explicit criteria.

The assessment instrument developed by Baird (1984) in the USA has shown greatest consistency in predicting serious future criminal behaviour by young people (see Table 9.1 below). It has been used extensively in the USA to determine the intensity of community supervision appropriate for convicted juveniles. It is based upon an analysis of research into those factors in a young person's social environment which are most closely associated with reconviction. Interestingly Baird does not include the seriousness of the current offence as an assessment criterion since, as (Clear, 1988) suggests, in the case of serious offenders 'current offence seriousness is not highly correlated with, and is often inversely related to, a negative outcome of community supervision'.

The points given to an offender are added together to derive a total risk score, with higher scores indicating a greater likelihood of further offending. Usually the range of possible scores is divided

Table 9.1 Baird's juvenile probation and aftercare risk assessment
instrument

Age at first ajudication
  0 = 16+
  3 = 14 or 15
  5 = 13 or younger   _____

Prior criminal behaviour
  0 = 0
  2 = 1
  4 = 2+   _____

Institutional commitments or placements of 30 days or more
  0 = 0
  2 = 1
  4 = 2+   _____

Drug/chemical abuse
  0 = none known or no interference with functioning
  2 = yes and some impact upon functioning
  5 = chronic abuse and/or dependency   _____

Alcohol abuse
  0 = none known or no interference with functioning
  1 = occasional abuse with some impact on functioning
  3 = chronic abuse with serious impact on functioning   _____

Parental control
  0 = generally effective
  2 = inconsistent and/or ineffective
  4 = little or none   _____

Behaviour in school
  0 = attending and achieving at a reasonable level
  1 = problems of attendance, punctuality or conduct handled
      effectively by school
  3 = severe truancy or behavioual problems
  5 = not attending/excluded   _____

Relationships with peers
  0 = good support and positive influence
  2 = negative influence, companions involved in delinquent behaviour _____
  4 = part of a group consistently involved in crime and violence

---

into three ('low' , 'moderate' or 'high' likelihood of reconviction)
and these categories are then translated into an indicated level of
community supervision.

Baird's assessment instrument does not offer failsafe predictions about future criminality. It is just one tool amongst many with which to link young people in trouble to interventions and programmes which, in terms of their intensity and sensitivity, will have a positive impact upon their lives and their life chances.

What really works?

James Howell is director of Research and Programme Development at the Office of Juvenile Justice and Delinquency Prevention in the US Department of Justice. In 1995, he and his colleagues published the results of a protracted and complex meta-analysis of literally thousands of youth crime prevention and treatment programmes in North America and Europe (Howell *et al.*, 1995). It is probably the most exhaustive study of its kind ever undertaken. They conclude that there are certain 'crucial themes', or characteristics, which occur again and again in the most successful and carefully evaluated programmes.

The key characteristics of effective interventions

- They are *holistic* (or *comprehensive* or *multi-systemic*), dealing with many aspects of youth's lives simultaneously, as needed.
- They are *intensive*, often involving multiple contacts weekly or even daily with at-risk youths.
- They mostly – although not exclusively – operate *outside the formal juvenile justice system*, under a variety of auspices: public, non-profit, or university.
- They *build on youths' strengths* rather than focusing on their deficiencies.
- They adopt a *socially grounded approach* to understanding a youth's situation and dealing with it, rather than a mainly individual or medical–therapeutic approach.

Howell *et al.* commend a theoretical eclecticism combined with a willingness to innovate and a commitment to sustained involvement with these young people for as long as it takes. As their colleague Terence Thornberry observes:

given its long-term persistent quality, it may be quite unreasonable to expect a short-term intervention to provide any effective remediation for this form of behaviour. But that is precisely what traditional programmes attempt to do . . . short-term programmes simply have too much to overcome to be successful. (1995, p.235)

The key components of effective interventions

Altschuler and Armstrong (1984), building on Howell's principles, suggest that effective programmes will contain several or all of the following 15 components:

- continuous case management,
- emphasis on reintegration and re-entry services,
- involvement in programme decision making,
- clear and consistent consequences for misconduct,
- enriched educational and vocational programmes,
- a variety of forms of individual, group and family counselling matched to the young person's needs which include opportunities for young people to discuss childhood problems,
- opportunities for success and the development of positive self-image,
- opportunities for the development of links between young people in trouble and pro-social adults and institutions,
- frequent, timely and accurate feedback for both positive and negative behaviour,
- strategies to reduce the influence of negative role models,
- a forum in which young people are enabled to recognise and understand thought processes that rationalise negative behaviour,
- programme components which are flexible enough to meet the needs of each individual young person,
- opportunities to engage with problems and deficits which got the young person into trouble in the first place,
- an underlying developmental rationale,
- attempts to alter 'ecological' or 'institutional' situations by working to improve family functioning, relationships in and with the school, and opportunities for productive and meaningful work.

This analysis points to the reality that successful rehabilitative endeavours tend to be undertaken by thoughtful people who are offered the freedom to use a variety of methods of intervention in ways which seem sensible in the light of the predicament of the young offender, available resources and new knowledge. Effective rehabilitative ventures are reflexive rather than prescriptive, they respond to situations as they unfold. Their language is an innovative dialogue, not a didactic monologue. However it is also clear that the types of criminality prevention programmes to which this analysis points could not be undertaken within the confines of the relatively brief community-based penalties specified by the Crime and Disorder Act (1998). It follows that, in the UK context, they are likely to be provided under the auspices of the corporate community safety strategies developed by local authorities and, in many cases, with the voluntary and not-for-profit sectors.

A cautionary note

The primary goal of tertiary, or criminality, prevention is to develop an intervention which eliminates, or at least reduces, the offending of the young people with whom we work. As has been suggested, this requires flexibility and a willingness to think through the nature of the problem to which we are attempting to devise a response, rather than relying upon some of the formulaic prescriptions for action which are currently on offer.

A minority of the young people who become involved with the youth justice system have committed violent or sexual offences and may themselves have been the subjects of violence or abuse. The process by which an abused person becomes an abuser, or the childhood victim of violence a violent offender, may well be explicable in terms of a psychological defence mechanism whereby the victim of aggression 'identifies' with the 'aggressor'. Identification with the aggressor, it is sometimes argued, enables the abused individual to repress the feelings of terror and vulnerability engendered by their abuse and violation.

To the criticism that, although young women are far more likely to be abused than young men, hardly any young women go on to become abusers, proponents of this position would reply that, as a result of differential gender socialisation, young women are far more likely to internalise the experience, developing feelings of self-blame, worthlessness, self-hatred, and sometimes expressing this through self-harm. Young men, by contrast, are far more likely to act the experience out.

Whatever one may think of this explanation, it is at least as plausible as those which suggest that violent or sexually abusive behaviour is a learnt behavioural pattern which is triggered by criminogenic social cues, or that it is a product of 'cognitive lag', a circumstance in which the abuser cannot think straight and is therefore unable to choose the right course of action (Ross *et al.*, 1988).

Speculation about the aetiology of particular behaviours is one thing, but responding to them is another, and this is, as it were, the crunch. If the first account of the aetiology of violent and sexually abusive behaviour is correct, interventions which attempt to confront that 'offending behaviour' will be saying to the perpetrator:

> You are a pretty hard and dangerous bloke. What you have done has caused you and a lot of other people a great deal of harm. You have caused suffering and heartbreak to your victim and their family and unless you knuckle down and work on alternative behaviours you will remain a hard and dangerous bloke and our only option will be to take you out of circulation.

Now this is music to the ears of anybody who is locked into a pattern of identification with their abuser, because here is an important official of the criminal justice system confirming that they are as powerful as they so desperately want to be.

This raises serious questions about whether 'offence-focused work', in which the young person's identity as a perpetrator of violent or sexual offences is emphasised at the expense of their identity as a survivor of such abuse, and reinforced in the process, is at all useful. An alternative approach would return with the young person to the site of their abuse and violation to enable them to take hold of the unacknowledged feelings bubbling under the surface in the present. The task would be to acknowledge these feelings, to help reconstruct an identity as a whole and valuable person, and so transcend the experience of abuse.

10

Custody

The implementation of the Criminal and Disorder Act (1998) alongside the planned expansion of secure and custodial provision looks likely to lead to an increased use of custody by the youth courts. This expansion threatens to dilute further the educational and rehabilitative resources available to young prisoners, making the task of developing penal regimes which, at the very least, do not worsen the problems which brought young people into custody in the first place, even harder.

A report from the Chief Inspector of Prisons (1998) on the conditions under which young offenders are held in Werrington Young Offender Institution, states the problem starkly.

I . . . find it quite incredible that the Prison Service should have thought it appropriate to remove tolerable although not ideal arrangements for the treatment of children in custody in favour of utterly unsuitable conditions, replacing dormitories not with small house blocks, but one, large new cellular houseblock, of the type being put up in adult prisons. To compound this, immediately the new accommodation was built, the population was increased and now 192 children are confined in 96 single cells designed for adults, on four landings of one long building. But what is even worse, and for which I can only assume that the Prison Service will plead the demands of overcrowding, because it cannot possibly be claimed to be providing appropriate custodial treatment and conditions for children, senior management failed to provide sufficient, or appropriate, resources to go with the increased numbers. To find children no longer eating together, but forced to take their food back to their cells, which are little more than lavatories, to eat, being limited to two evenings of association in a week, on landings where there are no chairs, so the time amounts to little more than an hour and a half standing outside rather than inside a cell, would be bad enough if found in any juvenile establishment. To find that adult prison conditions have been deliberately introduced, overturning previous and appropriate treatment and conditions for children, is nothing short of disgraceful.

In its final report on the 'juvenile secure estate', the government's Youth Justice Task Force (1998) considered the arrangements for detaining young offenders in young offender institutions (YOIs) run by the prison service, secure accommodation run by local authorities, and the Glenthorne Youth Treatment Centre run by the Department of Health. The Task Force concluded:

> 36. The different types of facilities for young people that constitute the secure estate are in need of major reform. Current arrangements are both inconsistent and unsatisfactory. Young offender institutions are too large. Bullying and abuse of one young offender by another occurs too often, while the education offered is often poor. Some young offender institutions, notably Lancaster Farms, have made major efforts to provide good services but even in these cases there is scope for improving links between the supervision a young person receives inside the institution and the supervision provided when the young person returns to the community.

Barriers to the successful implementation of rehabilitative programmes within custodial institutions for young people

As we have noted, cognitive–behavioural approaches to rehabilitation are currently popular within the UK prison system and other custodial institutions. However, like many other rehabilitative programmes before them, they fail to take cognisance of the factors which are most likely to undermine their success, namely the anti-rehabilitative or anti-therapeutic effects of the institutional culture and the mismatch between the inmates and their micro-social milieu.

The anti-rehabilitative effects of institutional culture

Maxwell Jones (1968) was one of the first people to recognise that institutional cultures could, and usually did, overwhelm even the most sophisticated therapeutic programmes operating within those institutions. As a result, he developed the idea of a *therapeutic community*, founded upon the principles of communication, democratisation and reciprocity, and designed to counteract anti-therapeutic institutional tendencies. 'This was a model upon which the successful regimes at the Barlinnie Special Unit in Scotland and Grendon Underwood prison in England were constructed.' One of the most important effects of such regimes is to render the usually opaque sub-cultures of staff and inmates transparent, and subject to discussion, scrutiny and decision by all members of the institution. As such, the entire institutional experience, rather than isolated sessions, constitutes the therapeutic or rehabilitative element of incarceration. This process has been shown to reduce intimidation and violence at all levels of the institution and to transform the inmate/offender from a passive subject to an active agent of the therapy or rehabilitation. As such, the inmate does not simply learn the skills they must acquire for a conforming life within and beyond the institution, they live them. It appears that skills and insights gained in this way are more readily transferable to other, non-institutional, settings than knowledge inculcated didactically for one or two hours a week in an otherwise unchanged institutional setting.

The mismatch between inmates and their milieu

Research by Brill (1978) indicates that work with disturbed or 'dangerous' young people in a residential or custodial setting is most effective when the regime is geared to what he describes as their 'conceptual level'. The idea of conceptual level does not refer to intelligence but, rather, the capacity of an individual to cope with the complexities of their social environment. Brill argues that, in the process of normal human growth and development, people move through a series of 'conceptual levels' and, as a result, are able to cope with social relationships of growing complexity. He identifies four levels of development (see Table 10.1), but notes that those people who are institutionalised or emotionally damaged will often fail to progress beyond, or may regress to, a relatively low conceptual level. He found that people who operated at levels B/C and B survived reasonably well in a situation in which they were asked to cope with the type of environment designed for people operating at level A. People operating at level A who had to undertake the degree of abstract reflection and self-determination appropriate to people operating at level C reacted in extreme and sometimes violent ways. However, when conceptual level A people were matched to level A environments, they coped very well. Beyond this, however, Brill found that level A people placed in level A environments tended to *develop*, suggesting that conceptual levels were not fixed but that inappropriate matching with a worker or an environment could retard or reverse this development. The implications of Brill's findings for UK prisons, which contain a disproportionate number of neglected, abused and institutionalised people, are that, contrary to the prescriptions of currently popular cognitive – behavioural programmes, one size does not fit all, and far greater attention must be paid to the fit between the inmate and the institutional and rehabilitative regimes into which they are inserted.

There are two major justifications for instituting regimes which strive to modify the milieu in which the inmate lives, neither of which

Table 10.1   Brill's conceptual levels

A.	Self-centred; unorganised; difficulty in planning; impulsive; limited control of emotions; easily confused; do not work out alternatives; cope with difficulties by denial; egocentric; reactive to authority.
B.	Learning ground rules and social norms which apply to everyone; think in terms of good/bad, right/wrong; categoric thinking; rely on external standards; dependent on authority; concerned with rules; frequently opposed to change.
B/C.	Learning about self and how one is distinct from others. Start to generate own concepts; some conditional thinking; reliance on internal standards and emotions; take into account two or more viewpoints simultaneously; deal with greater ambiguity; more assertive but not necessarily by aggression; interpersonal differentiation; can adapt to change.
C.	Applying self-controls to an empathetic understanding of other persons and differences between them.

relies on the possibility that such regimes would equip inmates with the skills to lead a law-abiding life beyond the institution, although this might well be the case. Firstly, such regimes have been shown to act as a bulwark against personal deterioration and the consolidation of the inmate's criminality while in gaol (Jones *et al.*, 1992).

Reactions to imprisonment for both men and women may range from a reckless determination to fight the system every inch of the way, on one hand, to silent withdrawal on the other. Whatever the strategy, the danger of personal deterioration in terms of institutionalisation, depression, detachment from reality or over-identification and adoption of a 'convict' persona, are ever present.

Secondly, they can serve as a protection against, and an alternative to, the institutional lawlessness which currently characterises the prison system in the UK.

The post-release element of the detention and training order

As we noted in Chapter 4, a DTO will be imposed where the offences in question are so serious that 'only custody is justified'. For 10- and 11-year-olds, the government maintains, the power to make an order would be exercised only in response to persistent offending, and only where the court considers that a custodial sentence is necessary to protect the public from further offending. For 12–14-year-olds, the DTO may be imposed only in relation to persistent offending. For 15–17-year-olds, it will be available for any imprisonable offence sufficiently serious to justify custody under the 1991 Criminal Justice Act.

The Home Office locates the individual *sentence plan*, constructed by prison officers in conjunction with a member of the youth offending team at the centre of effective pre- and post-sentence release supervision. However no mention is made of the contribution the prisoner might make to the plan. It is important to remember that post-release supervision constitutes part of the penalty imposed on the young person and may well mean that many of them will be at least ambivalent about having to work with us, and possibly quite resistant to doing so. Nonetheless it is not unreasonable to assume that, if they are party to the construction of the sentence plan, they will be more likely to comply with it. It is intended that the sentence plan will inject greater coherence into the work of both the YOTs and the prison officers involved with the prisoner, and greater continuity between work undertaken in the prison and after release.

The Probation Service *National Standards* which currently govern young offender institution throughcare (to be replaced in the fullness of time by *YOT National Standards*) identify 'protection of the public', 'prevention of reoffending' and 'successful reintegration into the community' as the primary objectives of throughcare. It is, however, reasonable to assume that the public is best protected if reoffending is reduced and successful reintegration into the community is achieved. This will be more likely if the personal deterioration which, as we have noted, often afflicts people who are confined to prison, can be ameliorated and prisoners' families, who often suffer great emotional and material stress as a result of the imprisonment of a partner or parent, can be supported.

We can therefore identify five key elements in the pre- and post-release supervision task:

1. reducing the risk of further offending,
2. minimising personal deterioration,
3. assisting and working with prisoners' families,
4. assisting resettlement in the community, and
5. preparing pre-discharge and home circumstances reports.

In terms of government policy and the stated objectives of the YOTs, reducing the risk of further offending appears to be the key throughcare task. If we are working with the young person on the issue of future offending we will usually be working on their attitudes, their behaviour, or both. We will usually be working with the young person towards an acknowledgement that they did, in fact, commit the offence(s) for which they were sentenced. It should be noted, however, that if the young person maintains that she or he did not do it and, as we know from experience, some of them really did not, then this approach will not work. Assuming that they acknowledge the offence(s), the worker will probably explore the fact that their offence(s) had consequences for the victims and that their conviction and sentence had consequences for them and those closest to them.

The worker will undoubtedly also raise the problem that, were the young person to commit similar offences in the future, they might well be arrested, prosecuted and imprisoned again, not least because they are now much better known to the police. This seemingly straightforward encounter with reality is often very difficult to facilitate because of the very understandable tendency of our clients to defend themselves psychologically against any guilt they might experience and the grim reality of their predicament. This is done by denying, or clinging to a distorted picture of, the actions which brought them to custody and the impact of those actions upon themselves and others. Imprisonment compounds this tendency by placing together, in a confined space, people who share nothing but the fact that they are not very good at getting away with crime. Having failed at it in real life, they often elaborate a fantasy of criminal success in order to keep up with the proverbial Joneses in the next cell.

Challenging young offenders about their view of, and attitudes towards, offending can be uncomfortable for them and for us, but change often involves a great deal of discomfort. This said, the worker must chart a careful course between a confrontation which debilitates the young person with guilt and remorse or, alternatively, drives them into a stonewall denial, and an approach which skates over the important questions and changes nothing. As in many other personal social welfare areas, active listening, empathy, reflection and the sensitive use of non-verbal cues constitute the basic skills of interpersonal work in post-release supervision. In sum, the worker is working towards a recognition on the part of the offender that they had, and have, a choice in the way they live their lives.

As we have noted, research undertaken in Germany by Speiss (1989) focused upon the relationship between reoffending and the circumstances of the offender in the areas of accommodation, income, addiction and personal relationships. He found, in the case of serious young offenders who had previously served prison sentences, that if, in the first 12 weeks of supervision in the community, supervisees had, with the assistance of their probation officers, managed to stabilise their financial situation, find a decent place to live, stabilise their addiction and maintain or extend their social relationships, there was a high probability of successful completion of the order and subsequent rehabilitation. Probation interventions which concentrated on these areas of social functioning were particularly effective with probationers/supervisees who had previously committed serious offences and served custodial sentences. He writes:

> In the case of positive change in social conditions during proba-
> tion, the correlation between severity of prior convictions and
> later recidivism was reduced to zero.... Even for the high risk
> groups of young recidivists, empirical evidence shows that prog-
> noses must not be based in a static way on past and unchangeable
> predictors like the number and severity of previous convictions;
> it could be improved on probation, while imprisonment would
> have added one more negative predictor without allowing for
> any positive change. (Speiss, 1989, p.32)

Mental health, addiction, desperation and child care

While it is a minority of young people, subject to throughcare, who experience mental health problems and problems of addiction, it is a sizeable minority. This problem has been exacerbated by the community care policies of the 1980s. Home Office research into suicides in Young Offender Institutions found that one-third of sentenced young offenders and one-third of those on remand were suffering from a diagnosable mental health problem. An earlier study by Gunn (1991) indicated that 17 per cent of adult male prisoners, 19.9 per cent of imprisoned male youths and 32.6 per cent of female prisoners had been diagnosed as suffering from psychoses, neuroses or personality disorders. It is estimated that between 10 per cent and 15 per cent of the clients supervised by one metropolitan probation service suffer from clearly identifiable psychiatric disorders.

A study in Northamptonshire in 1982 found that 47 per cent of clients had an alcohol-related problem (Harding, 1987). In a review undertaken by the Inner London Probation Service in 1989 it emerged that a minimum of 30 per cent of the clients of the service had a drink or drug problem which had a serious impact on their propensity to offend. In one area, 50 per cent of clients had serious problems of addiction. It must be stressed that this is a minimum figure. The review did not consider clients who were addicted to other legal substances and it was based on information which, in the case of addiction to illegal drugs, required clients to incriminate themselves by revealing it. Neither did it include excessive drinking or drug taking which did not appear to have a bearing on offending (ILPS, 1991).

In addition to those who are addicted or 'mentally ill' there are those who are constrained by poverty and circumstance. Of the people supervised by the ILPS in the early 1990s, 59 per cent were unemployed, with 40 per cent of them reporting serious financial problems. Then there are the growing numbers of young people who leave local authority care to find that they are not only homeless but involved, against their will, in the crime of vagrancy, and the homeless and rootless young men and women who becoming involved in prostitution in order to survive. Some, at least, of the young people who are subject to *throughcare* will be parents, and those who are will have very young children, the welfare of whom any YOT worker who reads the newspapers will have firmly in mind.

These are the people who constitute the lion's share of throughcare caseloads and what evidence we have suggests that neither the Crime and Disorder Act's commitment to symbolic punishment nor its cognitive – behavioural technology will have a great deal of relevance to their plight. A realistic response will require different skills and different knowledge. It will require the judgement and emotional resilience to live with the uncertainty and anxiety which work with such troubled people generates.

References

Altschuler, D. and Armstrong, T. (1984) 'Intervening with Serious Juvenile Offenders', in Mathias, R. (*et al.*) (ed.), *Violent Juvenile Offenders*, San Francisco, National Council on Crime and Delinquency.

Audit Commission (1996) *Misspent Youth: Young People and Crime*, London, Audit Commission.

Baird, S.C. (1984) *Classification of Juveniles in Corrections: A Model Systems Approach*, Madison, WI, National Council on Crime and Delinquency.

Barberan, J.M. (1997) 'Mediation in Spanish Youth Justice, *Social Work in Europe*, vol. 3, no. 3.

Berry, S. (1984) *Ethnic Minorities and the Juvenile Court*, Nottinghamshire Social Services Department.

Blagg, H. and Smith, D. (1989) *Crime Penal Policy and Social Work*, London, Longman.

Bohn, I. (1996) 'Action Against Aggression and Violence', *Social Work in Europe*, vol. 3, no. 1, pp. 32–6.

Bottoms, A. and McWilliams, W. (1979) 'A Non-treatment Paradigm for Probation Practice', *British Journal of Social Work*, 9, pp. 159–202.

Box, S. and Hale, C. (1986) 'Unemployment, Crime and the Enduring Problem of Prison Overcrowding', in Matthews, R. and Young, J. (eds), *Confronting Crime*, London, Sage Publications.

Bratton, W. (1997) 'Crime is Down in New York: Blame the Police', in Dennis, N. (eds), *Zero Tolerance, Policing a Free Society*, London, Institute of Economic Affairs.

Bright, J. (1991) 'Crime Prevention: the British Experience', in Stenson, K. and Cowell, D. (eds), *The Politics of Crime Control*, London, Sage Publications.

Brill, R. (1978) 'Implications of the Conceptual Level Matching Model for Treatment of Delinquents', *Journal of Research in Crime and Delinquency*, 12, pp. 229–46.

Burney, E. (1979) *Magistrate, Court and Community*, London, Hutchinson.

Campbell, B. (1993) *Goliath: Britain's Dangerous Places*, London, Methuen.

Capra, F. (1982) *The Turning Point*, London, Flamingo.

Centre for Educational Management (1997) *Learning From Failure*, London, Roehampton Institute.

Chester, R.L. (1994) 'Flying Without Instruments or Flight Plans: Family Policy in the United Kingdom', in Dumon, W. (ed.), *Changing Family Policies in the Member States of the European Union*, Brussels, Commission of the European Communities.

Clarke, R. (1980) 'Situational Crime Prevention: Theory and Practice', *British Journal of Criminology*, vol. 20, no. 2, pp. 136–47.

Clear, T. (1988) 'Statistical Prediction in Corrections', *Research in Corrections*, 1, 1–39.

Cohen, S. (1979) 'The Punitive City', *Contemporary Crisis*, vol. 3, no. 4, pp. 341–63.

Cooper, A., Hetherington, R., Baistow, K., Pitts, J. and Spriggs, A. (1995) *Positive Child Protection: A View From Abroad*, Lyme Regis, Russell House Publishing.

Crawford, A. (1998) 'Delivering Multi-agency Partnerships in Community Safety', in Marlow, A. and Pitts, J. *Planning Safer Communities*, Lyme Regis, Russell House Publishing.

Cullen, E. (1992) 'The Grendon Reconviction Study, Part 1', *The Prison Service Journal*, 90, pp. 35–7.

Currie, E. (1991) 'International Developments in Crime and Social Policy', in NACRO (ed.), *Crime and Public Policy*, London, NACRO.

De Liege, M-P. (1989) 'The Fight Against Crime and Fear: a New Initiative in France', in Hope, T. and Shaw, M. (eds), *Communities and Crime Reduction*, London, HMSO.

De Liege, M-P. (1991) 'Social Development and the Prevention of Crime in France: a Challenge for Local Parties and Central Government', in Farrell, M. and Heidensohn, F. *Crime in Europe*, London, Routledge.

Dennington, J. and Pitts, J. (1991) *Developing Services for Young People in Crisis*, London, Longman.

Dennis, N. (ed.) (1997) *Zero Tolerance: Policing a Free Society*, London, IEA.

Department of Health (1989) *The Children Act*, London, HMSO.

Elejabarrieta, F. *et al.* (1993) *Els Programes de Mediacio: Que Pensen i Com Els Viuen Les Parts Implicades*, Barcelona Universitata Autonoma de Barcelona.

Elliott, D., Huizinga, D. and Morse, B. (1986) 'Self-reported Attendance: a Descriptive Analysis of Juvenile Offenders and their Offending Careers', *Journal of Interpersonal Violence*, 1, pp. 472–515.

Esping-Andersen, G. (1990) *Three Worlds of Welfare Capitalism*, Cambridge, Polity Press.

Etzioni, A. (1994) *The Spirit of Community: The Reinvention of American Society*, New York, Touchstone.

Fagan, J.A. (1991) *The Comparative Impacts of Juvenile and Criminal Court Sanctions on Adolescent Felony Offenders* (Final Report, Grant 87-IJ-CX-4044, to the National Institute of Justice), Washington, DC, US Department of Justice.

Farrington, D. (1996) *Understanding and Preventing Youth Crime*, York, Rowntree.

Farrington, D. and West, D. (1993) 'Criminal Penal and Life Histories of Chronic Offenders: Risk and Protective Factors and Early Identification', *Criminal Behaviour and Mental Health*, 3, pp. 492–523.

Feeley, M. and Simon, J. (1992) 'The New Penology: Notes on the Emerging Strategy of Corrections and its Implementation', *Criminology*, vol. 30, no. 4, pp. 452–74.

Feld, B. (1987) 'The Juvenile Court Meets the Principle of the Offense: Legislative Changes in Juvenile Justice Statutes', *Journal of Crime Law and Criminology*, 78, pp. 471–533.

Feld, B. (1993) 'Criminalising the American Juvenile Court', in Tonry, M. (ed.) *Crime and Justice: An Annual Review of Research*, Chicago, University of Chicago Press.

Forrester, D., Frenz, S., O'Connell, M. and Pease, K. (1990) *The Kirkholt Burglary Prevention Project: Phase II*, (Paper 23), London, Home Office Crime Prevention Unit.

France, A. and Wiles, P. (1996) *The Youth Action Scheme: a Report of a National Evaluation*, London, Department for Education and Employment.

Gallo, E. (1995) 'The Penal System in France: From Correctionalism to Managerialism', in Ruggerio, V., Ryan, M. and Sim, J. (eds), *Western European Penal Systems: a Critical Anatomy*, London, Sage Publications.

Ginsberg, N. (1992) *Divisions of Welfare*, London, Sage Publications.

Graham, J. (1988) *Schools, Disruptive Behaviour and Delinquency*, London, Home Office.

Graham, J. and Bennett, T. (1995) *Crime Prevention Strategies in Europe and North America*, New York and Helsinki, European Institute for Crime Prevention and Control.

Graham, J. and Bowling, B. (1995) *Young People and Crime*, London, Home Office.

Gunn, J. (1991) *Meeting the Need*, London, Home Office.

Hagan, J. (1993) 'The Social Embeddedness of Crime and Unemployment', *Criminology*, 31, pp. 455–91.

Hagell, A. and Newburn, T. (1994) *Persistent Young Offenders*, London, Policy Studies Institute.

Hall, S., Crichter, C., Jefferson, T., Clarke, J. and Roberts, B. (1978) *Thatcherism*, London, New Left Review.

Harding, J. (ed.) (1987) *Probation and the Community*, London: Tavistock.

Hargreaves, D. (1967) *Social Relations in the Secondary School*, London, Routledge & Kegan Paul.

Hirschfield, A. and Bowers, K. (1998) 'Monitoring, Measuring and Mapping Community Safety', in Marlow, A. and Pitts, J. (eds), *Planning Safer Communities*, Lyme Regis, Russell House Publishing.

Home Office (1990) *Crime, Justice and Protecting the Public*, Cmnd. 965, London, HMSO.

Home Office (1991) *Safer Communities: the Local Delivery of Crime Prevention Through the Partnership Approach*, London, HMSO.

Home Office (1992) *National Standard for Pre-Sentence Reports*, London, HMSO.

Home Office (1995) *National Standards for the Supervision of Offenders in the Community*, London, HMSO.

Home Office (1997) *No More Excuses*, London, HMSO.

Home Office (1998a) *The Crime and Disorder Act*, London, HMSO.

Home Office (1998b) *Report of the Chief Inspector of Prisons on Werrington Young Offender Institution*, London, Home Office.

Home Office (1998c) *Aspects of Crime, Youth Offenders*, London, Crime and Criminal Justice Unit Research and Statistics Directorate, Home Office, June.

Hope, T. (1994) 'Communities, Crime and Inequality in England and Wales', paper presented to the 1994 Cropwood Round Table Conference, *Preventing Crime and Disorder*, 14–15 Sept., Cambridge.

Hope, T. and Foster, J. (1992) 'Conflicting Forces: Changing the Dynamics of Crime and Community on a Problem Estate', *British Journal of Criminology*, vol. 32, no. 92.

Howell, J., Krisberg, B., Hawkins, D. and Wilson, J. (eds) (1995) *Serious, Violent & Chronic Juvenile Offenders: a Sourcebook*, London, Sage Publications.

Hudson, B. (1985) 'Sugar and Spice and All Things Nice', *Community Care*, 4 April.

Hutton, W. (1995) *The State We're In*, London, Jonathan Cape.

ILPS (1991) *Demonstration Unit Data on Addiction Amongst Probation Clients*, London, ILPS.

ILYJS (Inner London Youth Justice Services) (1995) *Statement of Principles and Practice Standards*, London, NACRO.

Jones, A., Kroll, B., Pitts, J., Smith, P. and Weiss, J. (1992) *The Probation Handbook*, London, Longman.

Jones, M. (1968) *The Therapeutic Community*, Harmondsworth, Penguin.

King, M. (1989) 'Social Crime Prevention ala Thatcher', *The Howard Journal*, 28, pp. 291–312.

King, M. and May, C. (1985) *Black Magistrates*, London, Cobden Trust.

Krisburg, B. and Austin, J. (1993) *Reinventing Juvenile Justice*, London, Sage Publications.

Lawrence, M. (1983) '. . . It's Different for Girls . . .', *Eureka, Journal of the London Intermediate Treatment Association*, Autumn.

Lea, J. and Young, J. (1988) *What is to be Done About Law and Order* Harmondsworth, Penguin.

London Youth Justice Managers Group (1998) *Report on the Remand Rescue Initiative at H.M. YOI/RC Feltham*, Report of Meeting 28/4/98.

McGahey, R. (1986) 'Economic Conditions, Neighbourhood Organisation and Urban Crime', in Reiss, J.A. and Tonry, M. (eds), *Communities and Crime*, Chicago, University of Chicago. Press.

Mandelson, P. and Liddle, R. (1996) *The Blair Revolution*, London, Faber.

Marlow, A. and Pitts, J. (eds) (1998) *Planning Safer Communities*, Lyme Regis, Russell House Publishing.

Martinson, R. (1974) 'What Works? Questions and Answers About Prison Reform', *The Public Interest*, Spring. 22–54.

Mathiesen, T. (1964) *The Defences of the Weak*, London, Tavistock.

Matza, D. (1964) *Delinquency and Drift*, New York, Wiley.

Menzies Lyth, I. (1960) 'A Case Study of the Functioning of Social Systems as a Defence Against Anxiety', *Human Relations*, vol. 13, no. 2.

Messerschmidt, J.W. (1993) *Masculinity and Crime: Critique and Reconceptualisation of Theory*, Maryland, Rowman & Littlefield.

Messner, S. and Rosenfeld, R. (1994) *Crime and the American Dream*, Belmont, CA: Wadsworth.

Mika, H. and Zehr, H. (1997) *Fundamental Concepts of Restorative Justice*, Harrisonburg, VA, Mennonite Central Committee USA.

Millham, S., Bullock, R. and Hosie, K. (1978) *Locking up Children: Secure Provision Within the Child Care System*, London, Saxon House.

Mills, C.W. (1959) *The Sociological Imagination*, Harmondsworth, Penguin.

Morris, A., Giller, H., Szued, M. and Geech, H. (1980) *Justice for Children*, London, Macmillan.

Murray, C. (1994) *The Underclass: the Crisis Deepens*, London, Institute of Economic Affairs.

Murray, C. (1997) *Does Prison Work?*, London, Institute of Economic Affairs.

NACRO (1987) *Diverting Juveniles From Custody*, London, NACRO.

National Association for Youth Justice (NAYJ) (1996) *Policy and Practice Guidelines for Youth Justice*, London, NAYJ.

Olweus, D. (1989) 'Bully/Victim Problems Amongst School Children: Basic facts and Effects of a School-Based Intervention Programme', in Rubin, K. and Pepler, D. (eds), *The Development and Treatment of Childhood Aggression*, Hillsdale, NJ, Erlbaum.

Page, D. (1993) *Building for Communities: a Study of New Housing Association Estates*, York, Joseph Rowntree Foundation.

Parker, H., Sumner, M. and Jarvis, G. (1989) *Unmasking the Magistrates*, Milton Keynes, Open University Press.

Parti Socialiste Français (1986) *Les murs d'argent. Manifeste contre la privatisation des prisons*, Paris, Parti Socialiste.

Pawson, R. and Tilley, N. (1997) *Realistic Evaluation*, London, Longman.

Pearson, G. (1987) *The New Heroin Users*, Oxford, Blackwell.

Picard, P. (1995) *Mantes-la-jolie: Carnet de Route D'une Mairie de Banlieue*, Paris, Syros.

Pitts, J. (1988) *The Politics of Juvenile Crime*, London, Sage Publications.

Pitts, J. (1995) 'Public Issues and Private Troubles: A Tale of Two Cities', *Social Work in Europe*, vol. 2, no. 1, pp. 3–11.

Pitts, J. (1996) 'The Politics and Practice of Youth Justice', in McLaughlin, E. and Muncie, J. (eds), *Controlling Crime*, Sage Publications/Open University Press.

Pitts, J. (1997) 'The Political Economy of Child and Youth Prostitution', in Barrett, D. (ed.), *Child Prostitution in Britain*, London, The Children's Society.

Pitts, J. (1998) 'Dickens and Flaubert: a Tale of Two Housing Estates', *Soundings: a Journal of Culture and Politics*, 8, Spring, London, Lawrence & Wishart.

Pitts, J. and Smith, P. (1995) *Preventing School Bullying*, (Paper 63), London, Home Office, Police Research Unit.

Pollard, C. (1997) 'Short-term Fix, Long-term Liability', in Dennis, N. (ed.), *Zero Tolerance, Policing a Free Society*, London, Institute of Economic Affairs.

Porteous, D. (1998) 'Young People's Experience of Crime and Violence: Findings From a Survey of School Pupils', in Marlow, A. and Pitts, J. (eds), *Planning Safer Communities*, Lyme Regis, Russell House Publishing.

Power, M., Benn, R. and Norris, J. (1972) 'Neighbourhood, School and

Juveniles Before the Juvenile Courts', *British Journal of Criminology*, 12, pp. 111–32.

Preston, R. (1980) 'Social Theology and Penal Theory and Practice: the Collapse of the Rehabilitative Ideal and the Search for an Alternative', in Bottoms, A.E. and Preston, H. (eds), *The Coming Penal Crisis*, Edinburgh: Scottish Academic Press.

Robbins, D. (1989) *Child Care Policy: Putting It In Writing*, London, HMSO.

Robinson, D. (1995) *The Impact of Cognitive Skills Training on Post-Release Recidivism Among Canadian Federal Prisoners*, Ottowa, Ottawa Correctional Services.

Ross, R., Fabiano, E. and Elwes, C. (1988) 'Reasoning and Rehabilitation', *International Journal of Offender Therapy and Comparative Criminology*, 32, pp. 29–35.

Rowntree Foundation (1996) *The Future of Work: Contributions to the Debate*, York, Joseph Rowntree Foundation.

Rutherford, A. (1986) *Growing out of Crime*, Harmondsworth, Penguin.

Rutter, M. and Giller, H. (1983) *Juvenile Delinquency: Trends and Perspectives*, Harmondsworth, Penguin.

Rutter, M., Maughan, B., Mortimore, P., Ouston, J. and Smith, A. (1978), *Fifteen Thousand Hours*, London, Open Books.

Sampson, R.J., Raudenbush, S.W. and Earls, F. (1997) 'Neighbourhoods and Violent Crime: A Multi-Level Study of Collective Efficacy', *Science*, August, no. 277, pp. 1–7.

Satir, V. (1964) *Conjoint Family Therapy*, Palo Alto, Science and Behaviour Books.

Schlossman, S., Zellman, G. and Shavelson, R., with Sedlak, M. and Cobb, J. (1984) *Delinquency Prevention in South Chicago: a Fifty Year Assessment of the Chicago Area Project*, Santa Monica, CA: RAND.

Scull, A. (1977) *Decarceration*, New Jersey, Spectrum Books.

Segal, L. (1990) *Slow Motion: Changing Masculinities, Changing Men*, London, Virago Press.

Smith, C., Farrant, M. and Marchant, H. (1972) *The Wincroft Youth Project*, London, Tavistock.

Speiss, G. (1994) 'Diverting Away From Custody and Trial: The Terman Experience', *Social Work in Europe*, vol. 1, no. 2.

Sullivan, M. (1989) *Getting Paid: Youth Crime and the Inner City*, Ithaca, Cornell University Press.

Szymanski, L.A. (1987) 'Statutory Exclusions of Crimes for Juvenile Court Jurisdictions', unpublished, Washington. National Center of Juvenile Justice.

Taylor, W. (1982) 'Black Youth, White Man's Justice', *Youth in Society*, 14–17 November.

Thornberry, T. (1995) 'Violent Families and Youth Violence', Fact Sheet no. 21, Washington, DC: Office of Juvenile Justice and Delinquency Prevention.

Thornicroft, G. (1991) 'Social Deprivation and Rates of Mental Disorder', *British Journal of Psychiatry*, vol. 15, no. 8, pp. 475–84.

168 *References*

Thorpe, D., Smith, D., Green, C. and Paley, J. (1980) *Out of Care*, London, Allen & Unwin.

Tonry, M. (1997) '*Minority Crime and Imprisonment Patterns in Europe: Implications for European Integration*', paper delivered to the British Criminology Conference, 17 July, Belfast.

Whyte, W.H. (1943) *Street Corner Society, Chicago*, University of Chicago Press.

Wikstrom, T. and Loeber, L. (1997) 'Communities and Crime', in Tonry, M. (ed.), *The Handbook of Crime and Punishment*, New York, Oxford University Press.

Williamson, H. (ed.) (1995) *Social Action for Young People*, Lyme Regis, Russell House Publishing.

Willis, P. (1977) *Learning to Labour: How Working Class Kids Get Working Class Jobs*, London, Saxon House.

Wilson, J.J. (1994) 'The Future of the Juvenile Justice System, Can We Preserve It?', paper presented to the 21st National Conference on Juvenile Justice, Boston, MA.

Wilson, J.Q. (1975) *Thinking About Crime*, New York, Basic Books.

Wilson, J.Q. (1983) 'Crime and Public Policy', in Wilson, J.Q. (ed.), *Crime and Public Policy*, San Francisco, ICS.

Wilson, J.Q. and Kelling, G. (1982) 'Broken Windows', *The Atlantic Monthly*, March.

Wilson, W.J. (1987) *The Truly Disadvantaged: the Inner City, the Underclass and Public Policy*, Chicago, University of Chicago Press.

Wolfgang, I. (1982) 'Abolish the Juvenile Court System', *Californian Laywer*, 12–13 [17].

Young, J. (1998) 'Zero Tolerance: Back to the Future', in Marlow, A. and Pitts, J. (eds), *Planning Safer Communities*, Lyme Regis, Russell House Publishing.

Youth Justice Task Force (1993) *Final Report on the Secure Estate*, London, Home office.

Index